A SPORTING ALMANAC
FISHING

A SPORTING ALMANAC

FISHING

Photographs by the
Daily Mail

Gareth Thomas

First published in the UK in 2003
exclusively for
WHSmith Limited, Greenbridge Road, Swindon SN3 3LD
www.WHSmith.co.uk

Produced by Atlantic Publishing
All photographs © Associated Newspapers Archive
except those listed on page 128

A catalogue record for this book is available from the British Library.

ISBN 0 9545267 3 2
Printed in China

Len Armstrong fishing at Lowood Lake, Windermere

CONTENTS

Foreword 6

Introduction 8

A Brief History of Angling 10

Where to Fish 14

The Species 30

Competitive Fishing 90

Women and Fishing 102

A Fishing Miscellany 106

Conservation Etiquette and the Law 114

Angling and the Environment 116

Glossary of Terms 124

FOREWORD

Whilst fishing with hook and line was once a matter of survival for primitive man, angling has become one of our most popular recreational sports, and from humble technological origins, fishing now supports a whole industry of constantly evolving tackle, baits and other equipment, which itself provides ever changing techniques. There are however aspects of the sport which remain utterly timeless; from immersing oneself in nature with the opportunity for quiet contemplation, to the excitement and satisfaction of striking and landing a fish.

This book is not designed specifically as a technical handbook, though it does contain a host of tips and advice; rather it gives useful reference, including sections on the kinds of fishing offered by different locations, codes of practice for conservation, and an extensive guide to common species found in UK waters.

Containing statistics and numerous quotations on fishing, this book also gently caricatures some of the more amusing and unusual moments of this diverse and rewarding pastime.

INTRODUCTION

Today, fishing is enjoyed by literally millions of people across all social divisions, in many forms and in all kinds of environments, from canals, lakes and rivers to rocky shores, beaches and out in the open sea, and although some choose to specialise in hunting for large specimens of particular species, participate in competitions, or simply enjoy patiently waiting for any catch, anglers are united by many of the challenges and pleasures that fishing has to offer.

Broadly speaking however, there are three main disciplines in rod fishing or angling. Most obviously there exists the division between freshwater and sea fishing, but freshwater fishing is itself further divided into 'coarse' and 'game' fishing, whereby members of the salmon family, salmonidae, such as the Atlantic salmon, trout and grayling compose the group known as game fish, and the remaining freshwater species are regarded as coarse. Game fishing is also frequently referred to as fly fishing, as the most common methods involve using artificial flies or lures, whereas coarse fish are typically caught by means of bait fishing, that is, offering some foodstuff on a hook, be it bread, maggots or sweetcorn, for example. Game fish will however take baits such as worms from time to time, as indeed, some coarse fish will take artificial flies, but there are variations in tackle and techniques designed to target specific fish or best employed in certain circumstances, and thus many further divisions are sometimes made.

HARMONY WITH NATURE

Regardless of any such distinctions, there has perhaps never been a better time to become involved in fishing. Fishermen have typically always attempted to pursue their sport in harmony with nature, but now more than ever, anglers, water authorities, landowners and environmentalists are seeking to ensure that there are more, better managed and cleaner waters to which more people have easy access. Once-polluted urban waterways have improved with the decline of heavy industry and the adoption of more stringent regulations, numerous new stillwaters are being set up and maintained, and fish species are generally thriving and increasing in size. The quality and range of tackle has also improved vastly whilst becoming ever more affordable. It is true that commercial sea fishing has witnessed a decline in stocks in our oceans, but with continued codes of good practice by anglers in support of various environmental agencies, our

Coracle fishing on the River Severn in the 1930s

seas and shorelines are also cleaner than ever, and it is hoped that such measures will protect species of sea-dwelling fish for generations to come. It is therefore imperative that all fishermen abide by certain rules of conduct, and recognise that they have a role of responsibility to ensure the future enjoyment of both the environment and the sport of fishing itself.

A brief history of ANGLING

H omo Sapiens may count fishing hooks as being amongst the earliest of our tools, yet it is somewhat difficult to date precisely when they were first invented and harder still to identify when rods were first employed. We do know however, that rods were in use some four thousand years ago, and probably much earlier, man presumably realising that a line tied to a branch could provide greater reach from shore or bank and ease deployment of hook and line in otherwise inaccessible locations. Around two thousand years ago Roman writers reported the use of long, sectioned rods, and in 'De Animalium Natura', Claudius Aelianus provides what may be the first description of fishing with an artificial fly, detailing the fastening of feathers to a hook with wool.

FISHING IN LITERATURE

Whilst references to fishing may be cited throughout ancient times, from Egyptian art to Roman and early Christian writings, it is not until the advent of printing that we find the first English writing on the subject, Dame Juliana Berners' book, 'Treatyse of Fysshyinge with an Angle' of 1496, in which Berners describes a two or three piece wooden rod of at least six foot long, with a line of braided horsehair. She also describes twelve flies that were later taken up by Izaak Walton, some of which remain in use to this day.

In 1653 Walton provided perhaps the most famous work of fishing literature ever published, 'The Compleat Angler', by which time rods were around twenty feet in length, comprising up to eight sections, but up until the 18th century technical progress in terms of tackle was remarkably slow and although some basic reels came into use by 1726, this was not common practice. Horsehair lines remained in use, though with the addition of metal rings to rods, these lines became somewhat longer.

The development of reels came alongside advances in the textile industries, particularly in Nottingham where the centre-pin was created. The use of reels became much more viable as lines became stronger, produced from cotton and silk and braided by machine, and reel design itself was inspired by wooden bobbins. In turn reels allowed rods to become shorter. By the end of the 18th century, fully ringed rods with fittings for reels were commonplace and their manufacture had become industrialised. It was around the same time too, that the first

A coarse angler pictured in the 1950s, who travelled from London to Goring on a special anglers' train service.

fishing club was set up. It was based in Dagenham in Essex, and it is believed that Britain's youngest Prime Minister, Pitt The Younger could be counted amongst its members.

The next major design alteration in fishing was to come in the form of a change to the materials used to make rods themselves. As Britain began to import strong but flexible exotic woods such as lancewood and bamboo in the 19th century, the potential for strong but lightweight rods was realised and the performance of rods was greatly enhanced.

Fishing became more popular throughout the 19th century, not least as workers in industrial cities attempted to supplement their diet, but pollution began to take its toll and so taking advantage of the railways, anglers began to form groups and travel into the countryside where they were able to rent waters and support re-stocking. A further technical improvement came as the fixed-spool reel was invented by Holden Illingworth in 1905, again a development from the textile industry, and along with the centre-pin it remains one of the most popular types in use today.

GROWING POPULARITY

The popularity of angling for sport continued to grow throughout the 20th century, and as clubs grew larger and more numerous they continued to address issues of pollution and the regulation of fish stocks. The close season was introduced in 1923 in order that fish were able to reproduce naturally in sufficient numbers, and the Anglers' Co-operative Association formed in 1948 called upon users of the waterways to abide by laws regarding pollution. The 1940s also heralded the first fibreglass rods and braided nylon lines, but it was possibly the 1970s that bore witness to the most rapid and dramatic changes, particularly with regard to coarse fishing. Fibreglass was replaced in turn by carbon fibre or graphite, providing stronger and lighter rods that enabled longer casting, reels became lighter and monofilament nylon line became dominant. In fact the tackle business boomed, with all kinds of innovative equipment available, and bait became an industry in its own right. New fish were introduced which saw the focus shifting to carp fishing and the divisions between match and specimen fishing began to appear; clubs tended to become more match-orientated, while individuals, more and more of whom now had cars, travelled far and wide in search of bigger fish.

And so to today, where it might now seem that what was once so simple an occupation has become highly complex, for the explosion of interest in angling has not only resulted in what can at times seem a bewildering diversity to some, but also appears to threaten a diminishing resource. However, with care, everyone can share in the magic that once compelled our ancestors to dangle a hook in the most dubious of waters from time immemorial.

Opposite: Mr David Cooper with a 42lb salmon caught in the Forss river.
Below: Peter Barker catching salmon in 1993.

WHERE to FISH

COARSE, GAME AND SEA

Over the course of the following pages, we outline some of the many and varied fishing environments, from urban or rural canals, to vast stillwaters and offshore wrecks, providing details of the kinds of fish you are most likely to find in certain habitats, particular methods employed to catch them, and hints on locating fish by learning to read different waters, a technique known as watercraft. Of course, the best way to learn is through experience, but perhaps some of the information presented here might whet the appetites of newcomers to the sport, and yet remain of interest to the more experienced angler or general reader.

COARSE FISHING

Coarse fishing, that is, fishing for all UK freshwater fish other than members of the salmon family, offers amongst the most diverse environments for the angler, a wide variety of species to fish for and as such, many different techniques; however, even if you are targeting specific fish in a certain location, part of the pleasure of coarse angling is that you never know for sure what fish are going to bite!

CANALS

Canals represent very good places to fish, especially for beginners, generally holding good stocks of fish, being fairly consistent in design with easy access by means of a towpath and usually offering inexpensive day-tickets. They tend to hold large numbers of fish, mainly smaller species such as roach, rudd and perch which will congregate in the shallows of the nearside close to the towpath, but also larger fish like bream, tench, chub and big carp which favour the quieter waters of the far bank, usually seeking cover amongst aquatic vegetation or overhanging trees and shrubs, and anglers will often use a fishing pole to reach these sheltered swims. The deeper, central channels of canals frequently harbour large eels, and big pike and zander can also be found, particularly around features such as bridges, where small fish may gather. Light float tackle is preferable when attempting to catch small silvery fish such as roach, whilst ledgering is more appropriate for eels and larger bottom-feeding species. Predatory fish are usually caught by means of deadbaiting or with lures.

Opposite: A line of green umbrellas stretching for nearly a mile on the north bank of the Royal Military Canal, Kent as 80 anglers wait for the whistle blast to start their match.

Previous page: John Clarke, who plans to spend his retirement fly fishing.

STREAMS & RIVERS

Unlike canals, which tend to be quite regular in construction, streams and rivers will vary along their course, offering more varied features and habitats, from the cold pools of mountain streams, to the wider, warmer and more heavily vegetated stretches of lowland rivers. It is important to note too, that different species of fish prefer specific kinds of environments. Furthermore, seasonal changes will see fish exhibiting different behaviour in the summer and winter river.

Generally, most coarse fish will not be found in the higher reaches of streams and rivers, preferring the slower flowing and more food-plentiful lowland stretches, although barbel and dace will congregate in fast-flowing water. Most fish are likely to be attracted to areas where there is some shelter, either in the form of vegetation, hollows in the river bed or undercut banks, and a plentiful food supply, such as in 'creases', where fast water meets slow and food is brought down in the current. This is especially true in the case of larger fish which will expend less energy to feed. In summer, tench, chub, bream and carp may be found feeding amongst reeds and lilies close to the banks. In winter, when the water is colder and both bankside and aquatic vegetation

A fine chub taken from the River Severn in Shropshire.

is more scarce, creases and deeper pools are likely places for numerous species, whilst predatory fish such as pike will hide amongst the remaining reed beds.

Many anglers have also found that subsiding winter floodwaters offer excellent fishing, as the water will tend to be coloured a little by silt and mud, and therefore offer feeding fish more cover in open water.

STILLWATERS - LAKES, GRAVEL PITS & RESERVOIRS: LAKES

Lakes and other stillwaters can be more problematic in terms of finding good swims to fish, as natural food will usually be more widely distributed where there is no current. However, as with rivers, anywhere that offers shelter and food, such as reed beds, dense patches of lilies or underwater depressions will usually harbour fish. Margin fishing can be particularly effective in lakes, with roach, carp, catfish and predators such as pike and perch all frequently feeding in the shallows close to the bank or around islands, particularly where cover is provided by overhanging plants. It is worth looking for disturbances caused by fish in these areas, either at the water's surface where they may sometimes roll in the water or release streams of bubbles as they forage for food on the bottom, or amongst vegetation which large fish may disturb as they swim.

Fishing a large stillwater, such as this lake, can be productive in windy conditions. Carp especially have a habit of following the prevailing wind.

GRAVEL PITS

Gravel pits often contain very large specimen fish but can be even harder to read than lakes, as most of the features where fish gather will be submerged.   Gravel pit bottoms are typically very uneven and require mapping out by plumbing the depth with a weight. Doing so will reveal shallow areas, sharp drop-offs, gentle slopes and gravel bars, all of which can offer attractive habitats for various species. In windy conditions carp, bream and rudd will gather on the windward shore or at the sides of submerged bars to feed. In warm weather, shallow areas may well be populated with shoals of fry, attracting large perch, but fish in gravel pits will tend to be more nomadic, moving around in search of the best feeding areas. In colder weather fish will move into deeper water to keep warm.

RESERVOIRS

Like gravel pits, reservoirs often have quite uneven bottoms, especially if they have been created in valleys where there will also tend to be a natural current which may bring food or colour into the main body of water. Plumbing can be a useful technique before beginning to fish a reservoir, but it is also worth observing the lie of the land surrounding a large body of water, as sloping or sharply cut banks may indicate similar features beneath the surface.

A lone fisherman at sunset. Whilst fish may be harder to locate in large bodies of water, they will often have regular feeding times. Typically, dusk and dawn are the best times to fish for most species.

GAME FISHING

Game fishing refers to the pursuit of members of the salmon family, such as the Atlantic salmon, trout species, char and grayling, and can be performed both in rivers and in stillwaters, usually by means of fly-fishing rather than using bait. Migratory species can frequently be found in either environment, often travelling long distances up rivers to spawn in highland lakes and lochs, but there are also a number of stocked fisheries containing cultivated species, especially rainbow trout which are scarce in the wild.

Fly fishing for salmon from a boat on the River Tay, Scotland.

STREAMS & RIVERS

Streams and rivers have long been the preserve of traditional dry and wet fly-fishing techniques for salmon, brown trout and grayling, with the latter inhabiting clear, fast-flowing stretches, while salmon and trout have a tendency to lie-up in creases or in deep pools behind obstructions where the slack water offers some respite from the surrounding stronger currents. The fast, shallower areas may well contain fish in the early morning or evening, with fish moving into more sheltered spots such as undercut banks or deeper pools throughout the day. Depending on the technique being used, anglers will either be studying the surface for rising fish, or looking beneath it to find those feeding on insects and larvae mid-water.

On fast-flowing mountain streams, large boulders create deep pools of slack water where fish will rest and feed out of the strong current.

LAKES & RESERVOIRS

Above: Targeting trout from the bank.
Below: Colin McNee trout fishing from a boat on Rutland Water.

Lakes and reservoirs offer the angler a choice of approaches, and larger, open waters may often be fly-fished from boats rather than the bank. But regardless, the same problems exist in either case, that is finding the fish in very large stretches of deep water and selecting an appropriate technique to catch them depending on what depth they are feeding at. Commercial, stocked lakes however, may often be much smaller and offer cultivated fish that will take bait or flies more readily than their wilier, wild counterparts. On such lakes a stalking technique is often employed, where fish that can be seen feeding in the margins are deliberately, sometimes repeatedly targeted to induce a bite.

SEA FISHING

Of all angling disciplines, perhaps sea fishing might be regarded as the most challenging. Certainly the environment is vast and the elements can at times be unforgiving. In addition there is also a huge diversity of species and no guarantee as to what kind of fish one might catch, if any at all. Sea fishing also presents the angler with a range of locations, from the relative comfort of harbour walls, to harsher rocky shores and the open ocean.

Fighting to bring in a catch in the choppy water of Whitley Bay.

PIERS & BREAKWATERS

Many sea anglers will enjoy their first sea fishing experience from a pier or breakwater, and they are certainly good locations for a beginner, providing convenient access to fairly deep water without the need for chartering a boat or for distance casting. Many species can be caught from piers, and whilst they may not provide access to the biggest specimens, they are very often good places to acquire knowledge and experience. Summer is probably the best time to fish from such structures as large numbers of many different species are likely to be present close to the shore in warmer weather, piers providing them with shelter and good feeding places. Dogfish, flatfish, members of the cod family, eels, mullet and garfish can all be caught from piers and breakwaters, but mackerel are likely to be the most numerous and eager to bite.

Deal pier in Kent. Many angling clubs organise friendly matches from piers, but they tend to be sociable locations anyway, and good places to pick up tips from more experienced fishermen.

BEACHES

Windswept, heavy seas usually offer better beach fishing than you will find in calm conditions.

Open stretches of beach, be they sand or shingle, can appear quite desolate but nonetheless, can offer rewarding fishing. In the case of shingle beaches, few fish are likely to be caught very close to the shore where the stones are always in motion, but slightly further out, at perhaps 25-50 yards, shelves with steep banks will be formed by the tide, providing deeper, sheltered areas where crustaceans and small bait fish will gather, attracting larger species. Flat, sandy beaches may at first seem even more unpromising, but in the right weather conditions, when there is a great deal of surf to stir up food, fish will come very close inshore. In the summer months, pouting, whiting, rays and flatfish are all commonly caught from beaches, whilst winter can be a rewarding time to fish for cod.

ROCKY SHORES

Rugged, rocky coastlines may often seem quite daunting and dangerous places to fish, and safety should be of prime concern. Such areas should never be fished alone, and it is important to be aware of fast-rising tides and large waves. However, they are excellent places for catching many larger fish, usually being surrounded by deep water and gullies which harbour plentiful food supplies. Large bass, conger eels, dogfish, tope and cod are all frequent catches from rocky outcrops, and large wrasse are also common, often being fished for from the top or faces of sheer cliffs.

A prize-winning cod caught from a seemingly barren shoreline.

ESTUARIES

Estuaries can be fished either from the shore or by means of small boats and are highly underrated locations. Many species seem to have a tolerance if not a preference for brackish water, and flatfish, rays and eels will often reside in the rich feeding grounds that estuaries provide, with species such as bass following shoals of small prey fish close inshore and mullet even entering rivers to feed.

Further out, in large deep estuaries, fish will congregate at high tide where river channels carved in the sand and mud meet sea water and deposit food. It can therefore be a good idea to study estuaries at low tide to identify such features.

Estuary fishing as it used to be. Today a dinghy is more likely to be used than these coracles.

CHARTER BOATS -
OFF-SHORE WRECKS

Whilst most anglers are probably not lucky enough to own their own boats, a day's fishing on open water can usually be easily arranged, with most ports offering charter boat fishing for groups or individuals. Sometimes these boats will remain fairly close to shore, but as wreck fishing has become increasingly popular, more and more boats now offer trips to wrecks further offshore where large cod, ling and conger eels can all be found, along with black bream, rays and the larger flatfish species. Ledgering, and drifting with lures are probably the most popular techniques in these conditions.

A Porbeagle shark being brought aboard with a gaff off the North Devon coast. Nowadays, small sharks tend to be unhooked in the water.

THE SPECIES

COARSE FISH

BREAM

(Bronze bream) (Abramis brama) Family: Cyprinidae

RECOGNITION: Young bronze bream tend to be silvery and extremely thin, becoming more thick-set, humped and slimy with age, also darkening to a deeper bronze colour. Bream have a downturned mouth, and deeply forked tail.
AVERAGE WEIGHT: 4-7lbs. LIFESPAN: 15-20 years.
NATURAL DIET: Insect larvae, especially bloodworms, small insects and snails.
HABITAT / GOOD LOCATIONS: Bream favour deep stillwaters such as reservoirs or gravel pits, or slow-moving rivers and canals. Notable locations include the Norfolk Broads, the Severn, Great Ouse and the Thames.

There are two species of freshwater bream, silver and bronze, but silver bream are much smaller, usually only a few ounces in weight, and are far less widespread. Bronze bream are a medium-sized, shy, bottom-feeding fish and prefer to stay in deeper waters; however they are also sociable fish, shoaling in their hundreds at birth and, it is thought, remaining in a particular shoal for life, establishing and patrolling regular feeding routes. In certain areas such behaviour has enabled anglers to predict shoal movements and to catch large amounts of bream quite quickly, but in deep gravel pits, large or solitary bream can be much harder to find and land, becoming increasingly nocturnal in their feeding habits and often seeming to shun baits in favour of their natural food.

Previous page: Fisherman catching bream on the Thames in Richmond, Surrey

DACE

(Leuciscus leuciscus)   Family: Cyprinidae

RECOGNITION: Small and narrow, with a grey-green or brown back, silver flanks, white belly, grey dorsal fin and tail, and yellowy or pink lower fins. Dace also have yellow eyes and a small mouth.
AVERAGE WEIGHT: Around 8oz.   LIFESPAN: 10-12 years.
NATURAL DIET: Insects, worms, snails, leeches and tiny crustaceans.
HABITAT / GOOD LOCATIONS: Rarely found in stillwaters, dace prefer fast-flowing, clear streams and rivers. They are quite widespread, but more common in southern England, with the Hampshire Avon being a notable location.

The Dace is the smallest freshwater fish targeted by anglers in the UK, and specimens over 1lb are extremely rare, yet they can provide entertaining fishing, being active feeders even in cold conditions. In spring and summer dace feed predominantly at the surface of well oxygenated, fast-flowing rivers, though they will feed at various depths and can often be found near weir pools where fast-flowing water meets deeper slower water. The dace is sometimes mistaken for a small chub or roach, but is slimmer than both, lacking the red eyes of roach and having a more pointed head and smaller mouth than chub. Dace can also be distinguished from small chub by their concave, rather than rounded dorsal and anal fins.

ROACH
(Rutilus rutilus)   Family: Cyprinidae

RECOGNITION: Blue-green back, silver flanks and belly. Red eyes, red-orange fins, protruding upper lip.
AVERAGE WEIGHT: 6-8oz   LIFESPAN: 10-15 years.
NATURAL DIET: Insects and their larvae, aquatic snails and plants.
HABITAT/GOOD LOCATIONS: Widely distributed throughout the UK in rivers, canals and stillwaters, but particularly favouring chalk streams.

The roach is common, a good feeder and modest in size, and as such, it is very often the novice fisherman's first catch. In spite of their size and willingness to bite however, roach tend to put up quite a fight and larger specimens are often quite wily, being much more difficult to tempt. Typically a shoal fish, with the exception of the largest individuals, roach feed together in groups throughout the year regardless of temperature, and on warm days may surface-feed in shallows. In colder weather though they will be found much closer to the bottom and large roach will generally avoid the surface altogether. When spawning, the sociable roach often shoal with other species and frequently hybridize with bream and rudd; a true roach however, is usually discernible by its protruding upper lip and brighter fins.

Opposite: A fine roach taken by Dennis Burgess.

CHUB

(Leuciscus cephalus) Family: Cyprinidae

RECOGNITION: Large, well defined bronze or silver scales on flanks, darker back and red lower fins. The chub has a large head and mouth with white lips.
AVERAGE WEIGHT: 2-3lbs.
LIFESPAN: 10-12 years.
NATURAL DIET: Insects, worms, frogs, crustaceans and small fish.
HABITAT / GOOD LOCATIONS: Chub are widely found throughout the rivers of England, Scotland and Wales, but have also begun to thrive where they have been introduced in stillwaters.

Chub are extremely cautious fish, preferring to seek refuge amongst aquatic weeds, between submerged roots or beneath bankside vegetation, but young chub can often be found feeding in shoals in the shallower areas of rivers, frequently with other species of fish such as roach or dace, and hybrids are not uncommon. Chub are also particularly avid feeders with a varied diet and will take a variety of baits at various depths, day or night. However, as with most coarse species they are likely to be found at greater depths in colder conditions. Due to their timid nature, chub in shallow water should be approached carefully to avoid frightening them into hiding places, but chub will take fairly large baits and larger, mature specimens sometimes live out a solitary, predatory existence.

BARBEL

(Barbus barbus)   Family: Cyprinidae

RECOGNITION: The barbel is green-brown, with pink-orange or brown fins, a streamlined body and a long, rounded snout with two pairs of barbules.
AVERAGE WEIGHT: 6-8lbs.   LIFESPAN: 10-15 years.
NATURAL DIET: Insects, worms, plants, tadpoles and small fish.
HABITAT / GOOD LOCATIONS: Fast-flowing, gravel-bottomed rivers throughout the UK, notably the River Kennet, the Severn, the Dorset Stour and Great Ouse.

Barbel are long, muscular fish, adapted to bottom-dwelling in fast-flowing water, and although they sometimes seek shelter amongst vegetation or in deep pools, barbel tend to feed in clear, fast stretches of water, seeking out food from the gravel bottom. Their diet and feeding habits are quite variable, though in certain locations barbel favour particular spots and more regular feeding times. Generally, barbel will tend to take larger baits at night, and in winter will feed less aggressively; in highly coloured water after winter floods however, they are often stimulated to feed and will readily take large, fragrant baits such as cheese, luncheon meat or lobworms. Whilst tending to be comparatively light in relation to their size, the barbel is a powerful swimmer putting up a strong fight when hooked, and as they have become more widespread, they have become increasingly popular.

TENCH
(Tinca tinca) Family: Cyprinidae

RECOGNITION: Thick-set, with an olive-green to bronze back and gold-green flanks composed of tiny, slimy scales. The eyes are small and orange, and the lips thick with small barbules at the corners. The fins are large and rounded.
AVERAGE WEIGHT: 3-4lbs. LIFESPAN: 15-20 years.
NATURAL DIET: Insects, small crustaceans and molluscs, worms, especially bloodworms, and algae.
HABITAT / GOOD LOCATIONS: Very widely distributed across the UK in gravel pits, reservoirs, lakes, canals and slow-flowing rivers.

The tench is primarily a bottom-feeding species, seeking out its food by rooting around in silt or mud, and such behaviour often betrays the presence of a shoal of tench as they can be spotted by the streams of bubbles that they release whilst feeding, usually around the base of lilies or in reed beds. Tench can however, be taken mid-water and occasionally at the surface, often gathering quite close to the bank. Whilst tench will take a variety of baits and are quite predictable in their habits, feeding most readily at dawn, this becomes more difficult in gravel pits where feeding times vary considerably. In winter tench hardly feed at all and are unlikely to be caught except on the warmest of days, and then only with very small baits.

CARP

(Cyprinus carpio)   Family: Cyprinidae

RECOGNITION: Carp are deep-bodied with large, brassy scales, a long dorsal fin, and two long barbules on the upper jaw.

AVERAGE WEIGHT: 8-10lbs.   LIFESPAN: Around 40 years.

NATURAL DIET: Insects, worms, plants, snails and crustaceans.

HABITAT / GOOD LOCATIONS: Still or slow-flowing waters, though found in all types of freshwater habitat. The biggest carp are usually found in large reservoirs, gravel pits or private lakes.

The carp has become perhaps the most popular coarse fish amongst anglers in the UK since its introduction around the 1400s. True wild carp remain, but through selective breeding, a number of varieties now exist, such as the common, grass, mirror and leather carp, most of which can grow quite rapidly to over 30lbs. The carp is also extremely widespread, but favours stillwater where they will feed around vegetation, either rooting around the bottom often close to the bank, or feeding on weed or insects at the surface. Whilst such behaviour can make the carp easy to spot, they can also be quite wary, cunning fish, and this, coupled with their size and appetite has made them a favourite sporting fish. In addition to the varieties mentioned, there is a further species of carp, the crucian (Carassius carassius), which is much smaller, usually more golden or bronze in colour and lacking the barbules of other species. It will breed with other carp however, and hybrids are quite common.

PERCH

(Perca fluviatilis)   Family: Percidae

RECOGNITION: Olive-green back, becoming distinctly humped with age, with striped flanks, white belly and red lower fins. The most distinctive feature of the perch is its two dorsal fins, the first of which is spiny.
AVERAGE WEIGHT: 8oz-1lb.   LIFESPAN: 10-12 years.
NATURAL DIET: Worms, insects, crustaceans and small fish.
HABITAT / GOOD LOCATIONS: Perch thrive in all freshwater environments and are widely distributed across the UK, growing largest in bigger reservoirs and gravel pits.

Perch are exceptionally striking fish, with beautiful colouration and an impressive, spiked, leading dorsal fin which they raise when alarmed or hunting. The perch is mainly a predator, but will also eat dead animals. Like the pike, perch are highly aggressive and catch their prey in much the same way, using their camouflage to hide amongst reeds before ambushing them, but perch also chase small fish, biting at their tails to prevent them from being able to swim, before going in for the kill. Younger perch shoal in large groups and tend to populate shallows in the early morning on warm days, feeding on insects and fish fry, before retreating to deeper water. As they grow, perch tend to form smaller groups, perhaps partly because they often exhibit cannibalistic behaviour, becoming increasingly solitary with age, and also being more likely to be found at depth. On summer mornings though, adult perch will also feed in shallow water. Perch remain active feeders in winter, but then are to be found in much deeper water.

ZANDER

(Stizostedion lucioperca) Family: Percidae

RECOGNITION: Streamlined, with a grey-green back, gold flanks and a white belly. Zander have perch-like dorsal fins, very large eyes, and a large mouth with sharp teeth.
AVERAGE WEIGHT: 4-8lbs. LIFESPAN: 15-20 years.
NATURAL DIET: Insects, worms and small fish.
HABITAT / GOOD LOCATIONS: Found in slow-flowing, lowland rivers, canals and lakes, particularly in East Anglia, though large specimens have been found in the River Severn and at Coombe Abbey Pool near Coventry.

The zander is a member of the perch family, and is sometimes referred to as the pike-perch. It has a dorsal fin arrangement much like that of a perch, with two dorsal fins, the first of which is spined. Zander are typically much larger than perch however, and it would be difficult to confuse even a small one with a perch due to their differences in colour and general body shape. Zander are not a native species, being first introduced to the UK in 1878 at Woburn Abbey Lake, and then in 1963 rather controversially, into the Great Ouse Relief Channel. Since then they have spread quite rapidly, but are still limited in distribution compared to most species in UK waters. Like both perch and pike, zander are predatory, primarily feeding on smaller fish, hunting in packs when young, and becoming more solitary with age and size. As their large eyes suggest, zander are adapted for hunting in low light and are especially nocturnal in clear water. In cloudier water conditions, if it is not too cold, however, zander may feed throughout the day, usually following their prey into vegetation or other sheltered spots.

Coarse fisherman at Chibbs Pool, near the River Stour in Dorset.

PIKE
(Esox lucius)   Family: Esocidae

RECOGNITION: Long, olive-green body marbled with grey and yellow camouflage markings, reddish fins, and a flattened head with high-set eyes, a protruding lower jaw and many rows of sharp teeth.

AVERAGE WEIGHT: 8-12lbs.   LIFESPAN: 20-25 years.

NATURAL DIET: Fish, amphibians, small mammals and waterfowl.

HABITAT / GOOD LOCATIONS: Widespread in rivers, canals and stillwaters of various sizes. Large specimens have been caught from the Norfolk Broads, River Avon and the Llandegfed Reservoir in Wales.

The pike is the largest predatory fish in UK waters, with an unmistakably long, powerful head and body. However, despite its appearance, the pike is less of a hunter than an ambush attacker, tending to lie hidden amongst aquatic vegetation or in hollows, propelling itself towards its prey in a sudden burst of speed. Larger pike, which are almost always females, conserve energy by being predominantly scavengers, taking dead or dying fish, and dead-baiting is particularly effective for catching large specimens. Younger, smaller pike usually live off small, shoaling fish however, and as the pike is an aggressive and instinctive predator which will go for any passing fish or animal in sight that causes a disturbance, lures are also a favoured pike-fishing method. Pike are often caught at dawn, but tend to establish eating patterns in particular waters and may become inactive after periods of feeding. However, wherever smaller fish congregate, pike will not be far away and can reach a good size even in smaller rivers and streams.

Above: A 27lb Pike caught from a gravel pit in Suffolk in 1960.
Opposite: Ten-year-old Lawrence Mullane catches a 2lb Rudd at St Katherine's Dock beside Tower Bridge in 1971, helping to prove the GLC claim that the Thames was becoming less polluted.

RUDD

(Scardinius erythrophthalmus)   Family: Cyprinidae

RECOGNITION: Golden-yellow in colour with scarlet fins and orange-yellow eyes. Also recognisable by its protruding lower lip. With age, rudd become more bronze in colour and deeper-bodied.
AVERAGE WEIGHT: 12-14oz, though up to 2lbs. is not uncommon.   LIFESPAN: 10-12 years.
NATURAL DIET: Insects and larvae, worms and shellfish.
HABITAT / GOOD LOCATIONS: The rudd is most common in Ireland and increasingly less prolific elsewhere. In England, gravel pits in Cambridgeshire and Bedfordshire offer some good opportunities.

The rudd is a particularly beautiful fish and though similar to the roach in appearance, is usually more rich in colour, with a less-rounded body shape and a protruding lower lip. Some hybrids are almost impossible to discern from true rudd however. Like roach, rudd are shoal fish and spend sunny days feeding amongst aquatic vegetation in the shallows. They are more shy than roach though, and although are almost exclusively surface-feeders, will tend to avoid coming too close to the bank unless sheltered by overhanging vegetation. In winter, or in deeper waters such as gravel pits rudd will bottom-feed, but large ones are usually to be found mid-water.

WELS CATFISH
(Siluris glanis)   Family: Siluridae

RECOGNITION: The Wels catfish has a long, muscular, tapered body ending in a huge head and mouth, with two long barbules on the upper jaw and four shorter ones on the lower.
AVERAGE WEIGHT: 10-15lbs.   LIFESPAN: 30-40 years.
NATURAL DIET: Swan mussels and other invertebrates, fish, frogs, small mammals and waterfowl.
HABITAT / GOOD LOCATIONS: The Wels catfish is quite limited in distribution, mainly confined to deep, slow-flowing rivers, lakes and gravel pits in the south of England. The biggest specimens have been taken from Claydon Lake in Buckinghamshire and Withy Pool in Essex.

The Wels catfish is another imported species which was first introduced, as with the zander, at Woburn Abbey around 1880, before being released more widely. A native of central and eastern Europe, where they tend to live in huge rivers and can grow to vast sizes, and reputedly approach one hundred years old, the largest specimens in UK waters are still amongst the biggest of our coarse fish. However, due to a great deal of illegal stocking, the rod-caught record has been closed and it is likely too, that larger catfish exist than have, or ever will be landed with rod and line. Despite its tiny eyes the catfish prefers murky conditions, or feeds at night, emerging from the depths to scavenge and hunt in shallower water and eating almost whatever it finds, using a combination of its highly developed senses of touch, hearing, vibration and smell.

Right: John Leath on his first outing
of the new fishing season.
Opposite: Steve Bond carrying a
record 98lb catfish caught at Oak
Lodge fisheries in Essex.

EEL
(Anguilla anguilla)   Family: Anguillidae

RECOGNITION: Serpentine in appearence with a dark back, yellow-brown flanks and a lighter belly, eels also have long dorsal and anal fins which converge at the tail.
AVERAGE WEIGHT: 3-4lbs.   LIFESPAN: Around 20 years, though it is thought that many live much longer.
NATURAL DIET: Decaying animal matter, small fish and their spawn, frogs, worms, insects and shellfish.
HABITAT / GOOD LOCATIONS: Widespread in the UK in all waters, growing largest in infrequently fished stillwaters.

The freshwater eel is the same fish known to sea fishermen as the silver eel. Eels begin their lives in the Sargasso Sea and then migrate inland, sometimes taking many years, and travelling out of water for periods of time to reach land-locked stillwaters. Then, after perhaps six to twelve years, most eels return to the sea to spawn, changing to a much more silvery colour. Some eels remain in freshwater for life however, and these are liable to grow to considerable weights. Like catfish, eels are mainly nocturnal scavengers and they hide in deep holes or hollows during the day. Eels also favour hiding in foreign debris such as tree trunks or discarded shopping trolleys, and will feed close to their hiding places, emerging at night, particularly when it is humid.

BRITISH ROD-CAUGHT RECORDS - COARSE

Fish	lbs	ozs	dms	Year	Captor and Location
Barbel	6	8	8	2001	Steve Curtin,
					Adams Mill, River Great Ouse, Bedfordshire
Bream common bronze	18	8	0	2001	K Walker, Bawburgh Lakes, Norwich *
Bream silver	0	15	0	1988	D Flack, Grime Spring, Lakenheath, Suffolk
Carp	59	12	0	2001	Mark Toland, Conningbrook, Kent **
Carp crucian	4	8	0	2000	J Allen, RMC Summers Pit, Yately, Hants
Carp grass	36	8	0	2001	C Nash, Horton Church Lake
Catfish	62	0	0	1997	R Garner, Withy Pool, Henlow, Bedfordshire ***
Chub	8	10	0	1994	P Smith, River Tees, Blackwell, Co Durham
Dace	1	4	4	1960	J L Gasson, Little Ouse, Thetford, Norfolk
Eel	11	2	0	1978	Master S Terry, Kingfisher Lake, Nr Ringwood, Hants
Perch	5	9	8	2002	Dean Rawlings (Aged 11), Glebe Lake, Fringford
Pike	46	13	0	1992	R Lewis, Llandegfedd, Wales
Zander	19	5	8	1998	D Lavender, Fen Water, Cambs
Roach	4	3	0	1990	R N Clarke, Dorset Stour
Rudd	4	10	0	2001	Simon Parry, Freshwater Lake, Co Armagh, NI
Tench	15	3	6	2001	D Ward

* AWAITING ACCEPTANCE - 18lbs 15oz
** AWAITING ACCEPTANCE - 61lbs 11oz
*** LIST CLOSED 23rd OCTOBER 2000

Seventies champion angler
Peter Burton

Len Armstrong fishing at Lowood Lake, Windermere

GAME FISH

ATLANTIC SALMON

(Salmo salar) Family: Salmonidae

RECOGNITION: When the salmon enters freshwater it has a steel-coloured back and silver flanks with dark spots. As they spend more time in freshwater and get closer to spawning, males become more bronze with red-brown blotches and develop a prominently hooked lower jaw known as a kype. Females become more purple.

AVERAGE. WEIGHT: 6-8lbs, or up to around 20lbs, depending on how long they have been at sea.

NATURAL DIET: Salmon returning to freshwater do not feed, at sea they feed on small fish, molluscs and crustaceans.

HABITAT / GOOD LOCATIONS: Clear, usually fast-flowing rivers swollen by rain, in northern England, the West Country, Scotland, Wales and western Ireland, sometimes also entering lakes. The Tweed, Tay and Spey are notable locations, as is the Hampshire Avon.

The Atlantic salmon is a majestic-looking fish, and well revered for both its arduous lifestyle and fine flesh, though anglers are encouraged to return them in order to protect dwindling stocks. Salmon begin their lives in freshwater in spring, and may remain in river systems for up to four years, developing first into 'parr' and then becoming 'smolts'. At this stage, usually in May, they begin their downstream migration towards the sea where they remain for between one and three years before heading back to the rivers of their birth in the summer, in order to spawn in early winter. Considering that they do not feed in freshwater, it remains something of a mystery as to how and why the Atlantic salmon can be stimulated to take bait or fly presented by an angler, though curiosity and aggression have been suggested.

Opposite: Hugh Fish of the Thames Water Authority presents Russell Doig with a trophy in 1983 after he caught the first trout to be taken from the River Thames by rod and line in 150 years. Below: The first salmon to be caught in the Thames in the 1993 season.

SEA TROUT

(Salmo trutta)   Family: Salmonidae

RECOGNITION: As with salmon, sea trout are silver with a few dark spots when arriving from the sea, darkening as they approach spawning.
AVERAGE WEIGHT: 1-3lbs, into double figures depending on age.
NATURAL DIET: Insects and larvae, worms, snails and small fish.
HABITAT / GOOD LOCATIONS: Clear fast-flowing salmon rivers, in the West Country, Scotland, Wales, and western Ireland, as well as in Scottish lochs, but shore fishing for sea trout is gaining popularity.

Like the salmon, the sea trout is a migratory fish, developing in lochs and rivers before heading to the sea, and then returning to spawn in freshwater. Unlike salmon however, many do not spend such long periods at sea, or travel such distances, though more survive spawning and may return there afterwards, congregating in estuaries. A further behavioural difference is the trout's willingness to feed in freshwater, and although swollen rivers will encourage them, trout are undeterred by lower levels, and summer is perhaps the peak period. Fly-fishing clear, low water on moonless nights is generally reckoned to produce the best results. Whilst salmon and sea trout can be hard to distinguish, the rear corners of the mouth extend beyond the eye in trout, and their spots tend to be rounder than the more cross-shaped markings of salmon.

BROWN TROUT

(Salmo trutta)   Family: Salmonidae

RECOGNITION: The brown trout is almost identical in appearance to the sea-going variety, but can vary incredibly in colour, with silvery to brown or yellow flanks, often heavily marked with dark or red spots. On occasion these spots may be minimal and patterns seem to vary from habitat to habitat, though brown trout seldom have spots on their tails, making them easier to distinguish from rainbow trout.
AVERAGE WEIGHT: Wild brown trout average about 1lb, but cultivated fish from 2-10lbs are quite common and both types reach double figures.
NATURAL DIET: Insects, crustaceans and small fish.
HABITAT / GOOD LOCATIONS: Wild brown trout inhabit clean, fast-flowing waters throughout the UK, including chalk streams in the south of England, and can be found in Lake Windermere and Scottish lochs. Cultivated trout hot-spots include Rutland Water, Dever Springs and Carsington Water.

The brown trout is in fact the same species as the sea trout, sharing a common sea-bound ancestry, but the brown trout lives its entire life in freshwater, spawning amongst gravel in well oxygenated streams and rivers, but also doing well in Scottish lochs. However, there is also an artificially reared, 'cultivated' form which are stocked

in reservoirs and gravel pits where they generally attain greater weights than the true wild variety. In England and Wales wild brown trout have become increasingly scarce, suffering from pollution and inter-breeding with stocked fish, though there are those taking steps to protect these natural populations. Young brown trout feed mainly on insects and small crustaceans, but as they grow they often begin to eat small fish such as minnows, with the largest specimens preying on coarse fish and even becoming cannibalistic.

RAINBOW TROUT
(Oncorhynchus mykiss)   Family: Salmonidae

RECOGNITION: Bottle-green or grey-green back, light belly, and silvery flanks marked with a violet stripe from gills to tail, which becomes more intense as the fish approach spawning.
AVERAGE. WEIGHT: From 1-2lbs, up to 10 or 20lbs where stocked.
NATURAL DIET: Insects and their larvae, planktonic crustaceans, snails and fish fry.
HABITAT / GOOD LOCATIONS: Stocked in lakes and reservoirs throughout the UK, with a wild population breeding in the Derbyshire Wye.

The rainbow trout is native to the Pacific coast of North America but is easily farmed and has done well since being introduced to Europe due to its rapid growth, high tolerance of poorly oxygenated water, variable temperature, and its adaptable diet. These same reasons however, often make the rainbow unpopular in rivers as it is more competitive and aggressive than the native brown trout, and it is only really established as a wild species in the Wye. In private lakes and gravel pits rainbow trout can reach around 20lbs, but large farmed fish between 10 and 20lbs are also frequently introduced to such waters, where they will feed on whatever food is most abundant. In larger bodies of water, where the trout have reverted to natural feeding, they can be much more difficult to catch, becoming wary of certain flies.

ARCTIC CHAR
(Salvelinus alpinus)   Family: Salmonidae

RECOGNITION: Blue-green or olive-green back, olive flanks mottled with cream and reddish markings. When spawning the char's belly turns from cream to a bright orange or red.
AVERAGE. WEIGHT: Around 1lb, though increasing to around 6 or 7lbs in certain areas.
NATURAL DIET: Insects, snails, fish eggs and small fish.
HABITAT / GOOD LOCATIONS: Deep, glacial lakes.

The arctic char occurs in both migratory and sedentary, that is, non-migratory, forms in the colder waters of the Northern Hemisphere, with the sedentary form being found further south than its migratory relative, dwelling in glacial lakes in the UK, USSR and Europe. In the UK they are located in relatively high altitude lakes in Snowdonia, the Scottish Highlands and the Lake District. Once fished almost exclusively from boats by professional fisherman, the char is now sought for sport and is thought to be increasing in size due to feeding around stocked salmon. Although char often live very deep down, they can be taken at the surface when feeding on insects.

Opposite: Samuel Lytle fishing for brown trout on the River Hodder where the Yorkshire-Lancashire borders meet.

GRAYLING

(Thymallus thymallus)   Family: Salmonidae

RECOGNITION: The grayling is streamlined, and silver in colour with a purple-blue sheen. Perhaps the most distinctive feature is its large dorsal fin, also purple in colour, with darker spots and red edges. The mouth is small and the eyes relatively large. As with all members of the salmon family the grayling has an adipose fin between the dorsal fin and tail, but it is particularly understated.

AVERAGE WEIGHT: 12oz-1lb.

NATURAL DIET: Insects, larvae, snails, crustaceans, fish fry and small fish.

HABITAT / GOOD LOCATIONS: Grayling live in fast-flowing southern chalk streams, tributaries and rivers such as the Avon, Kennet and Frome, and also in Wales, northern England and around the Scottish borders.

Grayling are fairly small silvery fish, but their iridescent scales and sail-like dorsal fin make them an exceptionally beautiful species. Due to their spawning habits grayling are often thought of as a coarse species, despite being a member of the salmon family, and they share the protection of the coarse close season. At one time, however, grayling were thought of as a pest and removed from trout rivers along with such species as dace and chub, by means of electro-fishing. Now though, grayling are thought worthy of fishing for sport. Young grayling congregate in shoals, usually feeding at the bottom of fast-flowing stretches of water, for which they are well designed, being highly streamlined. They will feed at various depths though, and readily take insects from the surface, rapidly darting up from the bottom. As with dace, grayling also remain good feeders in winter, but will tend to find more sheltered areas to hide, as larger grayling will throughout the year. As grayling can only tolerate the cleanest water, they are fairly limited in distribution.

BRITISH ROD-CAUGHT RECORDS

GAME

FISH	LBS	OZS	DMS	YEAR	CAPTOR AND LOCATION
Char					
Natural	9	8	0	1995	W Fairbairn,
					Loch Arkaig, Inverness, Scotland
Cultivated					Vacant
Grayling					
Natural	4	3	0	1989	S R Lanigan,
					River Frome, Dorset
Cultivated					Vacant
Salmon (Atlantic)					
Natural	64	0	0	1922	Miss G W Ballantine,
					River Tay, Scotland
Cultivated					Vacant
Trout (Brown)					
Natural	31	12	0	2002	Brian Rutland,
					Lock Awe, Argyll, Scotland
Cultivated	28	1	0	1995	D Taylor,
					Dever Springs Trout Fishery, Hants
Trout (Rainbow)					
Cultivated	36	14	8	1995	C White,
					Dever Springs Trout Fishery, Hants
Resident	24	1	4	1998	J Hammond,
					Hanningfield Reservoir, Essex
Wild					Vacant
Trout (Sea)					
Natural	28	5	4	1992	J Farrent, Calshot Spit, River Test
Cultivated					Vacant

Trout fishing on the Whittaker, a tributary of the Tweed.

SEA FISH

COD AND LING

Cod
(Gadus morhua)   Family: Gadidae

RECOGNITION: Cod can vary considerably in colour, but are typically grey-green or brown with mottled flanks and back, pot-bellies and a large head and mouth with protruding upper lip. Cod also have a long barbule on the chin, three dorsal and two anal fins.
AVERAGE WEIGHT: 5-8lbs as young fish, to around 10-15lbs, but they do grow much larger.
NATURAL DIET: Lugworms, molluscs, crustaceans and fish.
HABITAT / GOOD LOCATIONS: Cod favour deep water but also frequent shorelines at high tide, and though present year-round and can always be caught at sea, in the south of England they are best taken from shores in winter.

Cod are highly valued as a commercial fish and are widespread around UK coastlines, but despite an ability to reproduce in large numbers, average sizes have fallen in recent years as a result of commercial pressure. When young, 'codling' as they are known, tend to spend time close to the coast, usually amongst kelp seaweed beds, and may adopt a red colouration, but as they grow cod will move further out to sea. Cod are mainly bottom-feeders, equipped with a huge mouth which enables them to eat all manner of invertebrates and small flatfish. Wrecks are a favoured spot for finding larger specimens.

Ling
(Molva molva)   Family: Gadidae

RECOGNITION: Similar to the cod in appearance, though usually darker, the ling shares the large mouth and barbule of the cod, but differs in its fin arrangement, having two dorsal fins, the second of which is particularly long, reaching almost to the tail. In fact the rear half of the ling is much more eel-like with a single, long anal fin and small tail.
AVERAGE WEIGHT: 10-30lbs.
NATURAL DIET: Mainly small flatfish.
HABITAT / GOOD LOCATIONS: Widely distributed around UK waters, though favouring clear water. The Cornish coast is a recommended location.

The ling is a close relative of the cod and shares many of the same traits in terms of both behaviour and appearance. The ling is however, far less likely to be taken from the shore, particularly in winter when they will remain at depth, but like cod, young ling spend some time feeding nearer to the coast. The adult ling are deep-water creatures which feed on crustaceans and fish around wrecks, often remaining motionless for many hours, venturing out from hiding places to hunt, but they are sometimes caught in deep water around rocky shorelines at weights of up to 20lbs.

Ling

Mature fish can grow to around six foot in length or longer, weighing 40-50lbs. Interestingly, the ling is also incredibly fertile, holding the record for the most eggs produced at one time amongst any vertebrates, which stands at an incredible 28,361,000.

POLLACK AND COALFISH

Pollack
(Pollachius pollachius) Family: Gadidae

RECOGNITION: Cod-like, green-brown with a well defined, dark lateral line and distinctive protruding lower jaw.
AVERAGE WEIGHT: 1-3lbs from the shore, increasing to around 12-16lbs in open water.
NATURAL DIET: Small fish and crustaceans.
HABITAT / GOOD LOCATIONS: Widespread around the UK coast, most prolific off the south-west coast.

Coalfish
(Pollachius virens) Family: Gadidae

RECOGNITION: Almost identical to the pollack, but lacking the protruding jaw and having a light-coloured lateral line, darker back and more rounded belly.
AVERAGE WEIGHT: Similar in size to the pollack, though heavier specimens have been caught from the shore.
NATURAL DIET: Small fish such as whitebait.
HABITAT / GOOD LOCATIONS: Widespread, though most common off the Scottish and south-western coasts.

Pollack and coalfish are both members of the cod family and are quite often found together, either around reefs and wrecks out at sea, where they usually feed on small fish in mid-water, or when young, feeding on crustaceans and sand eels from the bottom, in the shallower waters of estuaries. Following winter storms can be a very good time to catch coalfish near the shore. Both fish tend to spawn at some depth, from winter up until spring, and the eggs drift inshore where the young fish hatch and form shoals. Although very similar in appearance, and often mistaken for one another, pollack can be distinguished from coalfish chiefly by their protruding lower jaw and dark lateral line.

Pollack

BLACK BREAM
(Spondyliosoma cantharus)   Family: Sparidae

RECOGNITION: Black bream are similar in appearance to those found in freshwater, being deep-bodied and relatively thin. The back is blue-black, shaded into grey or silver flanks. The dorsal fin is large and spiny, and they have large eyes.
AVERAGE. WEIGHT: 1-2lbs. NATURAL DIET: Worms, crustaceans and small fish.
HABITAT / GOOD LOCATIONS: They are found throughout UK waters but specifically around south coast ports such as Littlehamptom.

Once confined to the south east-coast of Britain, black bream are found more widely, though in recent years, not in significant numbers, and this may be the result of overfishing. Large shoals of bream have a tendency to congregate off the south coast, over reefs, around May, before dispersing, but they can be found up until early autumn. Black bream are mainly bottom-feeding, but will feed mid-water over reefs, wrecks, and rocky ground. Smaller bream often come inshore, feeding around piers much later in the season

Opposite: Hundreds of anglers at Hastings Pier for the open international Sea Angling Festival.

POUTING AND WHITING
Pouting
(Trisopterus luscus) or (Gadus luscus)   Family: Gadidae

RECOGNITION: Copper-brown back, with an iridescent pink sheen on the flanks, and a cream underside. Pouting have a small barbule under the chin.
AVERAGE WEIGHT: Usually under 1lb from the shore, to around 2-3lbs at sea.
NATURAL DIET: Small molluscs and crustaceans.
HABITAT / GOOD LOCATIONS: Around piers, breakwaters, shores and estuaries, in greatest numbers around the south coast. Larger pouting will be found further out, typically over wrecks.

Whiting
(Merlangius merlangus)   Family: Gadidae

RECOGNITION: Similar in colour to the pouting but with more silvery flanks and a lighter belly. Whiting lack barbules.
AVERAGE WEIGHT: See pouting.
NATURAL DIET: Small fish.
HABITAT / GOOD LOCATIONS: Throughout UK waters, most commonly close to beaches, piers and breakwaters.

Pouting and whiting are small members of the cod family and both are most common close to the shore; in fact, whiting are the most commonly caught marine species in UK waters. Pouting spawn in late winter or spring, with whiting spawning in early summer, and autumn evenings at high tide can be a good time to fish for them from beaches or man-made structures such as piers or harbours. Both species occur in great numbers around the south and east coasts, but are also frequently caught in the Bristol Channel.

BASS

(Dicentrarchus labrax)   Family: Percichthyidae

RECOGNITION: Bass are muscular fish with dark backs and silver flanks, often with a pronounced lateral line. The mouth is large and the gill covers have sharp edges. Bass also have an eight or nine-spined leading dorsal fin, much like that of the freshwater perch.
AVERAGE WEIGHT: 1-3lbs as 'schoolies' or shoaling fish, with larger solitary specimens closer to double figures.
NATURAL DIET: Crustaceans, molluscs and small fish.
HABITAT / GOOD LOCATIONS: Generally shallow inshore waters around rocks or wherever there is a good deal of surf, but also found in estuaries.

The European sea bass is a relative of the perch and shares a similar spiky dorsal fin, but it is a much larger fish and a favourite amongst sea anglers for its striking appearance and powerful fighting ability. When young, bass form large shoals or schools and are often found very close to the shore preying on shoals of smaller fish such as herring and young mackerel, entering estuaries and even fresh water during spring tides. Larger more solitary bass may be found further out over reefs or other such features but they too will come close inshore whenever there is stormy weather or lots of surf disturbing crabs and small fish from their hiding places.

Opposite: A ferry in Kent takes anglers from the Prince of Wales Pier, Dover, to the Southern Breakwater.

MACKEREL

(Scomber scombrus)   Family: Scombridae

RECOGNITION: Mackerel are small, torpedo-shaped fish with blue backs striped with black, zebra-like markings. The flanks and belly are white, but covered in an iridescent film. Several tiny fins proceed from the rear dorsal and anal fins to the tail.
AVERAGE WEIGHT: 1lb.
NATURAL DIET: Plankton and fish fry.
HABITAT / GOOD LOCATIONS: Mackerel spend the winter in the depths of the Irish Sea and around the Channel Islands before beginning their migration inshore in vast numbers in spring, when they can then be caught all around the coastlines of the UK, but concentrated in the west.

Mackerel are relations of the tuna and look very much like miniature versions of them. They are also incredibly fast little fish, and very powerful for their size. After spawning at sea in spring huge shoals of mackerel head to our western coasts in search of food, mainly fry, in late spring and early summer, and will chase their prey right up to beaches, causing a frenzy as they break the surface. At such times many fish may be caught quite quickly, with light spinning tackle and lure or float-fished bait, but if they are to be used as bait themselves, several may be caught at a time with feathers and lures. In the autumn, smaller groups of larger mackerel may be found bottom feeding near the shore, but usually where the water is deepest, and ledgering may prove rewarding at evening high tides.

BALLAN WRASSE

(Labrus bergylta)   Family: Labridae

RECOGNITION: Deep-bodied, with a long, spiny dorsal fin, wrasse are usually olive-green in colour with an orange belly and markings, though they become more vividly coloured with age, looking distinctly tropical. Wrasse can also be identified by large teeth behind rubbery lips.
AVERAGE WEIGHT: 2-3lbs.
NATURAL DIET: Crustaceans and molluscs.
HABITAT / GOOD LOCATIONS: Widely found in UK waters, often close to piers and breakwaters or in deep water near rocks. Large wrasse are most abundant off the west coasts of the UK and Ireland.

Wrasse are highly unusual for many reasons, and perhaps strangest of all is the fact that they are all born as females, with some becoming male at around six years old. The wrasse also sleeps at night, often in crevices amongst the rocky outcrops at the foot of cliffs where it makes its home.

Ballan Wrasse

Wrasse feed on molluscs such as limpets which they strip from rocks with their highly specialised front teeth, and they also browse seaweed for small crabs which make good bait. Rocky coastlines offer the best wrasse fishing, and where the shore is least accessible, the largest specimens will be found. Wales, Devon and Cornwall are all good locations, but wrasse tend to be quite seasonal and are scarce in winter.

THICK-LIPPED GREY MULLET

(Chelon labrosus)   Family: Labridae

RECOGNITION: Solid, fully-scaled and streamlined, the mullet has a grey back and horizontally striped flanks. The mouth is small, but as its name suggests, thick-lipped.
AVERAGE WEIGHT: 2-3lbs, growing much larger in harbours and lagoons.
NATURAL DIET: Mainly microscopic organisms, algae, small molluscs and crustaceans, though mullet will eat a variety of food, including carrion, particularly around man-made structures.
HABITAT / GOOD LOCATIONS: Widespread in shallow water around the shores of the UK, in harbours, estuaries and lagoons.

Three species of grey mullet exist in UK waters, but the thick-lipped mullet is of most interest to anglers, and probably poses the greatest challenge. For whilst they can frequently be observed feeding tantalisingly near the surface, close to harbour walls and piers, they are often not very easy to catch. Mullet can be caught inshore for much of the year in certain locations, but usually spend the winter at greater depths. Throughout spring and summer however, shoals of mullet are common inshore, and seem to enjoy the more brackish water of estuaries, even venturing into river systems. They also enter harbours and inland lagoons, growing to double-figure weights where food is plentiful.

GARFISH

(Belone belone)   Family: Belonidae

RECOGNITION: Long and slender with a silvery blue-green back and silver belly. The garfish is rather eel-like in appearance but has a long toothy bill or beak.
AVERAGE WEIGHT: 12oz-1lb.
NATURAL DIET: Small fish fry.
HABITAT / GOOD LOCATIONS: Garfish prefer warm, clear water and are predominantly found off the south-west of the UK; they can however, be caught all along the south coast.

Garfish are known by various names such as garpike and needlefish, but also as the mackerel guide, and this may give us some insight into their behaviour. Garfish winter at sea, but when spring brings warmer weather they begin to come inshore with shoals of mackerel, feeding on fry just beneath the surface of the water. Garfish are related to flying-fish and at times may also be spotted leaping clear of the surface, a technique which they use to evade predators, and

Opposite: Jack Parker shows his catch, a 3lb cod, to admiring Deal children Rosemary Fairbairn, left, and Beverley Douglas.

when hooked they often exhibit this same behaviour, seemingly walking on their tails in an attempt to free themselves. As with mackerel, garfish can be caught from boats, beaches and piers throughout the summer, but sometimes are also found in estuaries.

SMALL FLATFISH
Dab
(Limanda limanda) Family: Pleuronectidae

RECOGNITION: Flat, with a rough, sand-coloured back, and smooth, pale underside. The lateral line curves around the pectoral fin.
AVERAGE WEIGHT: Just under 1lb.
NATURAL DIET: Seaweed, worms, crustaceans, molluscs and fish fry.
HABITAT / GOOD LOCATIONS: Inshore over sandy sea beds, widely distributed though perhaps more common in the south.

Sole
(Solea solea) Family: Cynoglossidae

RECOGNITION: Flat, and quite elongated, giving the sole an oval shape. Dull brown in colour with dark blotches and speckles and usually a completely white underside. Sole can also be identified by their rough texture and a dark patch on the uppermost pectoral fin.
AVERAGE WEIGHT: Around 1 lb.
NATURAL DIET: Worms, molluscs, crustaceans and fry.
HABITAT / GOOD LOCATIONS: Muddy, sandy or gravel beds close inshore around the UK, less common in the far north.

Dab and sole are amongst the smallest species of flatfish, and a frequent catch in shallow water from beaches, piers and breakwaters. They are usually present year-round, and in peak condition in the autumn months, becoming more scarce at the coldest times in winter. Sole particularly will retreat into the depths and enter an almost hibernation-like state. Though rarely achieving weights above 1-2lb, smaller fish such as dab and sole are often more plentiful, offering the potential for regular sport, and, as they are amongst the best-tasting flatfish, a good meal.

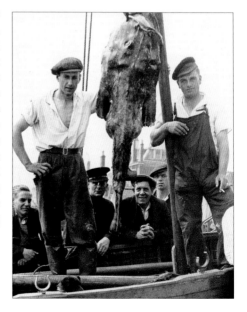

Two Deal fisherman with a 70lb angler fish in 1937. They lost their haul of dogfish because of ripped nets.

LARGE FLATFISH
Turbot
(Scopthalmus maximus)   Family: Bothidae

RECOGNITION: Large, diamond-shaped flatfish, with a white belly and scaleless mottled brown back covered with bony tubercles. The lateral line curves around the pectoral fin, and the turbot has a large mouth.
AVERAGE WEIGHT: 12-15lbs.   NATURAL DIET: Sandeels, small fish and crustaceans.
HABITAT / GOOD LOCATIONS: Estuaries, sandbanks and wrecks up to a depth of about 80 metres, with young fish being found much closer to the shore. Widespread, but more common in the south-west around Dorset and Devon.

Plaice
(Pleuronectes platessa)   Family: Pleuronectidae

RECOGNITION: Diamond-shaped flatfish with distinct orange or red spot markings.
AVERAGE WEIGHT: 3-6lbs.   NATURAL DIET: Mussels and other shellfish, crustaceans and marine worms.
HABITAT / GOOD LOCATIONS: Common inshore around sandbanks and estuaries. Widely distributed with good spots around both the south-west and east coasts.

Halibut
(Hippoglossus hippoglossus)   Family: Pleuronectidae

RECOGNITION: The largest of the flatfish, dark olive-green and lightly patterned, with smooth skin.
AVERAGE WEIGHT: Probably around 60-100lbs, though huge specimen of over 500lbs have been caught by commercial fishermen.
NATURAL DIET: Fish, including other flatfish.
HABITAT / GOOD LOCATIONS: Typically found in deep, cold water. In the UK they are concentrated around Scotland, the Shetland Isles and the Orkneys.

Most flatfish share common behavioural and physical traits, spending much of their time camouflaged on the sea bed eating crustaceans and smaller fish, and all are fished commercially for food. Of these species, the plaice is perhaps best known, most abundant and easily recognisable, but all are widespread around British shores, particularly in warmer waters around the more southerly regions. The halibut is something of an exception, growing to immense proportions and favouring very deep, cold waters. All flatfish begin their lives as 'roundfish' swimming upright in the water, feeding on plankton, small crustaceans and fry and taking larger prey as they grow. As they develop, flatfish undergo a remarkable transformation; the body flattens, they begin swimming on their sides, and the fish settles on the sea bed where one side of the skull grows disproportionately to the other, resulting in one eye and nostril migrating to the opposite side of their heads, so that both are on the uppermost side. The mouth also twists, and the fish then remain as bottom dwelling-species.

SKATES AND RAYS

Common Skate
(Raja batis)   Family: Rajidae

RECOGNITION: Flat, diamond-shaped body and long tail common to all skates and rays, with a grey, dark green or brown back, sometimes marked with spots and stripes. The underside is grey with black pores.
AVERAGE WEIGHT: Perhaps 60-100lbs, though much larger specimens have been caught by anglers.
NATURAL DIET: Fish, including dogfish, small rays, flatfish, crustaceans and other invertebrates.
HABITAT / GOOD LOCATIONS: Large skate are found over mud and sand, often at great depth, whilst smaller rays may be found closer to the shore.

Thornback Ray
(Raja clavata)   Family: Rajidae

RECOGNITION: Typical ray shape, usually sandy or grey in colour depending on the colour of the sea bed, covered with bony spines.
AVERAGE WEIGHT: 8-10lbs.
NATURAL DIET: Small fish and crustaceans.
HABITAT / GOOD LOCATIONS: Fairly shallow water, frequently feeding around estuaries. The Bristol Channel and Thames Estuary offer good fishing.

Stingray
(Dasyatis pastinaca)   Family: Rajidae

RECOGNITION: Thick body, usually olive-green or brown without markings, long whip-like tail ending in a venomous barb.
AVERAGE WEIGHT: 20-30lbs
NATURAL DIET: Mainly molluscs and crustaceans
HABITAT / GOOD LOCATIONS: Stingray tend to come inshore in warm weather, feeding above mud and sand in the shallower waters around estuaries, especially on the east coast.

Skates and rays are in fact members of the same family (with the term 'ray', generally being applied to the smaller species), and they are related to dogfishes and sharks, being cartilaginous fish with no true backbone. Skates and rays are flat, but unlike the group of fish known as flatfish, they do not undergo a developmental transition to become so, and thus display far greater symmetry. They are generally diamond-shaped with wing-like pectoral fins and long tails. Most are sandy-coloured and are speckled to provide camouflage as they rest on the sea bed, but colours vary according to their surroundings.

The thornback ray is the most common and widespread ray in British waters, and is also the most likely to be caught from the shore. The common skate however, unfortunately suffers something of a misnomer, for although they were certainly the most numerous skate species in our seas some twenty or thirty years ago, today these huge, deep-water fish are mainly to be found in the waters around south-west Ireland and the Scottish Islands and as with most large skates and rays are usually only caught from boats. The stingray is one of very few poisonous fish around the UK, equipped with a barbed tail that can cause serious injury and infection, and it is not uncommon to catch a specimen that has had its barb or tail previously removed. Stingray can grow quite large, up to around 70lbs, and it is interesting to note that they are viviparous, that is, they give birth to live young rather than producing eggs. Thornbacks on the other hand, produce the egg sacs found on beaches which are referred to as mermaids' purses.

Stingray

SHARKS AND DOGFISH
Blue Shark
(Prionace glauca) Family: Carcharhinidae

RECOGNITION: Long and slim, of typical shark shape, intensely blue back with a white underside. Blue sharks have long pectoral fins and a distinctive notched tail.
AVERAGE WEIGHT: 60-70lbs, but sharks over 200lbs have been caught around the UK.
NATURAL DIET: Herring, mackerel, dogfish and other fish.
HABITAT / GOOD LOCATIONS: Widely distributed, but most common off south-west England and Ireland.

Tope
(Galeorhinus galeus) Family: Scyliorhinidae

RECOGNITION: Tope are slim sharks with a grey-brown back and flanks, a white belly, pointed snout and two dorsal fins, the leading dorsal being larger. The pectoral fins are also large.
AVERAGE WEIGHT: 40lbs.
NATURAL DIET: Crustaceans, starfish, pouting, whiting and small cod.
HABITAT / GOOD LOCATIONS: The Thames Estuary and south-west coasts are favourable locations, with the Isle of Man offering good tope fishing from the shore in late summer.

Blue sharks and tope are amongst the largest species caught in British waters, and both are usually present only in the summer months. Blue sharks are common in tropical seas where they will grow to over twelve feet in length, and although most specimens found off UK shores will be about half this size, 200lb blue sharks have been caught here. Tope are smaller by comparison, but can grow to over seven foot long and weigh over 70lbs. Both tope and blue sharks are agile, strong and aggressive feeders and although tope tend to live and feed at depth, they have been known to feed at the surface as blue sharks do, attacking shoals of small fish such as mackerel. Both species are most likely to be caught from boats at sea but will come into the shallows to feed and can be taken from the shore. Blue sharks and tope are rarely taken for food or exhibition today, and as a result of this catch-and-release practice are thriving, providing welcome sport for many UK anglers.

Lesser Spotted Dogfish
(Scyliorbinus Caniculus) Family: Scyliorhinidae

RECOGNITION: Shark-like in shape but considerably smaller than other species. Lesser spotted dogfish have orangey backs covered in dark spots, cream undersides, and very rough skin.
AVERAGE WEIGHT: About 1lb.
NATURAL DIET: Crustaceans, starfish and small fish.
HABITAT / GOOD LOCATIONS: Close to the seabed over gravel, sand or mud. Found throughout UK waters but the Welsh coast is especially good.

Spurdog
(Squalus acanthius)   Family: Squalidae

RECOGNITION: An elongated, slender shark with grey back and flanks and a pale belly. Spurdog lack the protective membrane over the eyes present in most sharks and can also be identified by sharp spurs positioned on their dorsal fins.
AVERAGE WEIGHT: 10-12lbs.
NATURAL DIET: Small fish.
HABITAT / GOOD LOCATIONS: Spurdog are usually found at sea, in moderately deep water over sandy bottoms. The south-west coast of England and south Wales offer the greatest numbers.

Small sharks and dogfish were once rarely deliberately sought by anglers, but spurdog in particular can provide good sport. The lesser spotted dogfish is considerably smaller and quite easy to catch, readily taking bait close to the shore throughout the year whilst the larger spurdog is more likely to be caught from beaches in late summer and autumn when it comes inshore to give birth. Both species have small sharp teeth and should be handled with care, but not specifically for this reason. The lesser spotted dogfish is also known as the rough hound and it has very coarse skin like sandpaper, while the dorsal spines on a spurdog can inflict injury, both species having a habit of squirming and attempting to curl around the arm if not held firmly.

This 9ft, 120lb bue shark was caught in 1958 by Dr Norman Lorraine west of Eddystone, Cornwall.

EELS

Silver Eel

(Anguilla anguilla) Family: Anguillidae

RECOGNITION: Long and snake-like with dark backs, yellow or bright silver flanks and bellies. Silver eels often have large eyes and usually quite pointed snouts.
AVERAGE WEIGHT: 2-3lbs.
NATURAL DIET: The European eel does not feed when returning to the sea to spawn, but males often remain quite close to river mouths, feeding on crustaceans, small fish and carrion.
HABITAT / GOOD LOCATIONS: Estuaries and harbours.

Conger Eel

(Conger conger) Family: Congridae

RECOGNITION: Long and muscular, with grey or brown backs and pale undersides. The dorsal and anal fins are continuous around the body and have a black edge.
AVERAGE WEIGHT: Perhaps 15-20lbs inshore, but congers grow rapidly and fish between 60-100lbs are not uncommon.
NATURAL DIET: Molluscs, crustaceans and fish.
HABITAT / GOOD LOCATIONS: Most common in the south, with the largest congers being caught from wrecks.

The silver eel referred to by sea fishermen is in fact the very same species that is found in freshwater and is a migratory fish, which adopts a silvery colour upon entering the sea on its way to spawn and die. The tiny returning elvers, sometimes called glass eels or bootlaces, congregate in estuaries before entering freshwater and males often remain in the lower reaches of rivers and in estuaries, coming and going between fresh and saltwater until they too migrate. At this time they no longer eat, allowing their stomachs to shrink and reproductive organs to take their place.

Conger eels are a much larger species and can grow to almost twelve foot long, and over 100lbs in weight. Such huge specimens however, are not often encountered and are difficult to catch with rod and line. They are however, the stuff of legend, being powerful and fearsome-looking eels equipped with very sharp teeth. Many an angler has lost strong tackle to a big conger eel. Smaller conger are more frequent inshore, with the larger ones living at depth around wrecks, mainly off the west coast of Britain. Large fish have been caught close to the shore however, and even in river estuaries. There is some suggestion that conger are seasonal, but there are places where they can be caught year-round, particularly where winters are mild. Autumn is a good time to fish for them, and they will usually feed at night. Like the European eel, conger are migratory, and spawn only once in their lifetime.

Conger Eel

BRITISH ROD-CAUGHT
RECORDS -SEA

FISH	LBS	OZS	DMS	YEAR	CAPTOR AND LOCATION
Bass					
boat	19	9	4	1987	S M A Neill, Belfast Lough, NI
shore	19	0	0	1967	H Legerton, Canvey Island, Essex
Black Bream					
boat	6	14	4	1977	J A Garlick, over wreck off S Devon coast
shore	6	8	6	2001	Rosanne Guille, Creux Harbour, Sark, CI
Coalfish					
boat	37	5	0	1986	D Brown, south of Eddystone over wreck
shore	24	11	12	1995	M Cammish, Filey Brigg, Yorkshire
Cod					
boat	58	6	0	1992	Noel Cook, North Sea, off Whitby
shore	44	8	0	1966	B Jones, Tom's Pt, Barry, Glamorgan
Conger					
boat	133	4	0	1995	V Evans, from wreck, Berry Head, S Devon
shore	68	8	0	1992	M Larkin, Devil's Point, Plymouth
Dab					
boat	2	12	4	1975	R Islip, Gairloch, Wester Ross, Scotland
shore	2	9	8	1936	ML Watts, Morfa Beach, Port Talbot, Glamorgan
Lesser Spotted Dogfish					
boat	4	6	8	1994	G Griffiths, off Port Logan, Scotland
shore	4	15	3	1988	S Ramsey, Abbey Burnfoot, Kirkcudbright
Garfish					
boat	3	9	8	1994	A Saunders, Mount Bay, Cornwall
shore	3	4	12	1995	F Williams, Porthoustock, Cornwall
Halibut					
boat	234	0	0	1979	C Booth, Dunnet Head, off Scrabster, Scotland
shore	10	-	-		Qualifying weight
Ling					
boat	59	8	0	1989	J Webster, off Bridlington, Yorks
shore	21	10	0	1994	K Smith, Seasons Pt, Plymouth, Devon
Mackerel					
boat	6	2	7	1984	W J Chapple, off Penbeth Cove, Cornwall
shore	5	11	14	1982	M A Kemp, Berry Head Quarry, Brixham

Thick-lipped Grey Mullet

boat	10	1	0	1952	P C Libby, Portland, Dorset
shore	14	2	12	1979	R S Gifford, The Leys, Aberthaw, Glamorgan

Plaice

boat	10	3	8	1974	H Gardiner (Age 16), Longa Sound, Scotland
shore	8	6	14	1989	R Moore, Southbourne Beach, Bournemouth

Pollack

boat	29	4	0	1987	W S Mayes, Dungeness, Kent
shore	18	4	0	1986	C Lowe, Abbotsbury, Dorset

Pouting

boat	5	8	0	1969	R Armstrong, off Berry Head, Devon
shore	4	9	0	1991	R Andrews, Pembrook, Guernsey, CI

Thornback Ray

boat	31	7	0	1981	J Wright, Liverpool Bay
shore	21	12	0	1985	S Ramsay, The Ross, Kirkcudbright

Blue Shark

boat	218	0	0	1959	N Sutcliffe, Looe, Cornwall
shore	40	-	-		Qualifying weight

Common Skate

boat	227	0	0	1986	R Banks, off Tobermory, Inner Hebrides
shore	169	6	0	1994	G MacKenzie, Loch Roag, Isle of Lewis

Sole

boat	4	1	12	1993	M Eppelein, Great Bank, CI
shore	6	8	10	1991	N V Guilmoto, off Alderney, CI

Spurdog

boat	21	3	7	1977	P R Barrett, off Porthleven, Cornwall
shore	16	12	8	1964	R Legg, Chesil Beach, Dorset

Tope

boat	82	8	0	1991	R Chatfield, off Bradwell-on-Sea, Essex
shore	58	2	0	1982	R J White, Baggy Point, N Devon

Turbot

boat	33	12	0	1980	R Simcox, Salcombe, Devon
shore	28	8	0	1973	J D Dorling, Dunwich Beach, E Suffolk

Whiting

boat	6	12	0	1981	N R Croft, Falmouth, Cornwall
shore	4	0	7	1984	T Dell, Abbotsbury, Dorset

Ballan Wrasse

boat	9	7	12	1999	A Heart, off Jersey, CI
shore	9	1	0	1998	P Hegg, Portland, Dorset

COMPETITIVE FISHING

SPECIMEN HUNTING
and
MATCH FISHING

F or many, angling will always remain a pastime, a means of relaxing in the open air, perhaps escaping from the drudgery of the daily routine, and although most anglers certainly enjoy the sport of fighting to land a powerful or wily fish, and even favour pursuing particular species for these reasons, there are those for whom this is competition enough, pitting their wits and skills one-on-one against those of the fish, often being satisfied with any quarry they might land. However, there are also more competitive fishermen, usually experienced anglers, who chose to take up specimen hunting or match fishing, possibly following a desire fostered by the experience of losing an exceptionally large catch, or attracted to the challenge of testing their skills against those of fellow anglers. In either case, these anglers are perhaps encouraged by the abundance of information which has raised the profile of the sport; specialist magazines, videos and at the top end of the scale, the lure of sponsorship deals and financial reward.

SPECIMEN HUNTING

The specimen hunter might be said to be closer to the pleasure angler in many ways, and some would certainly not regard themselves as competitors, rather as attempting to fulfil their own goals by pursuing large specimens patiently and methodically. Increasingly, however, this area of fishing has gained popularity and there are competitions run by clubs and magazines for impressive specimens, with many of the best specimen hunters securing sponsorship from bait and tackle companies. There is of course also the accolade of entering the British record listings, and with many species increasing in size, perhaps due to global changes in weather, the improved conditions of much of our water systems and even baits provided by anglers, undoubtedly some specimen hunters are motivated by hoping to beat current records. It could be said too, that specimen hunters are often amongst the most dedicated, if not strictly competitive of anglers, for their specialisations tend to involve not only great preparation in terms of selecting tackle and honing their skills, but also in searching for and travelling to more distant locations for their quarry.

Catching specimen fish (larger than average) - Dr Bruno Broughton (opposite left) John Wells (opposite right), and Joseph Haywood (below) of Castle Gresley, Derbyshire with a record Pike caught in 1974.

MATCH FISHING

The majority of those who participate in angling matches or competitions become involved in the sport by joining a local fishing club and competing in inter-club leagues, perhaps entering larger open tournaments with the chance of larger prizes as levels of skill and confidence grow. Beyond this, the best club anglers might represent national teams, but at the highest level, match fishing also has its professionals, those picked from such teams to take part in world championships and who reap the highest rewards. Whatever level one aspires to, the way to start is to join a club.

The aim in coarse fishing matches, be they team or individual affairs is generally to catch the heaviest weight of fish within an allotted time period, and tactics will vary from venue to venue depending on what fish are available or biting from whichever 'peg', that is position, that one has been allocated. Certain species of fish may be ruled out and minimum weights sometimes also apply, therefore it pays to do some research into particular venues. There may also be a points system per-fish in operation, whereby one might have to decide upon either catching many small fish or fewer heavy ones. Regardless, speed is certainly of the essence and the practised match angler will have their casting and tackle changes down to a fine art.

Sea fishing matches, whether on or offshore, are usually performed on a 'roving' basis, where competitors' names are drawn at regular intervals and they are then free to take up a position of choice from which to fish. There are almost certainly likely to be minimum weight limits, and often separate points and prizes for overall weights and specimen-weight fish.

Left: The Benson and Hedges fly fishing championship begins on Rutland Water. There were 30,000 fishermen when the competition began but now only 60 boats and 20 teams compete for a place in the final. Opposite: When a river was stocked with 7,800 trout to open Missouri's fishing season, 1,900 anglers turned out. A number caught fish, others caught only other anglers. Below: Some of the 70 fishermen who cast their lines at a competition in Rochester, Essex. The nearest water and fish were five miles away.

COMPETITIVE CASTING

One final area of competitive angling that deserves a mention is that of casting competitions. Such events are governed by their own official organisations such as the British Casting Association and the UK Surf Casting Federation and are divided into both accuracy and distance trials, with and without weights. Usually being held on dry land so as to ease accurate measurement, these land-based events might make anglers look like fish out of water, but the aim is to encourage better casting and therefore more skilful fishing.

CHAMPIONSHIP STATISTICS

WORLD FRESHWATER CHAMPIONSHIPS (COARSE)

MEN'S INDIVIDUAL

1957	Mandeli (Ita)	1981	Dave Thomas (Eng)
1958	Garroit (Bel)	1982	Kevin Ashurst (Eng)
1959	Robert Tesse (Fra)	1983	Wolf-Rudiger Kremkus (FRG)
1960	Robert Tesse (Fra)	1984	Bobby Smithers (Ire)
1961	Ramon Legogue (Fra)	1985	David Roper (Eng)
1962	Raimondo Tedasco (Ita)	1986	Lud Wever (Hol)
1963	William Lane (Eng)	1987	Clive Branson (Wal)
1964	Joseph Fontanet (Fra)	1988	Jean-Pierre Fouquet (Fra)
1965	Robert Tesse (Fra)	1989	Tom Pickering (Eng)
1966	Henri Guiheneuf (Fra)	1990	Bob Nudd (Eng)
1967	Jacques Isenbaert (Bel)	1991	Bob Nudd (Eng)
1968	Gunter Grebenstein (FRG)	1992	David Wesson (Aus)
1969	Robin Harris (Eng)	1993	Mario Barras (Por)
1970	Marcel van den Eynde (Bel)	1994	Bob Nudd (Eng)
1971	Dino Bassi (Ita)	1995	Pierre Jean (Fra)
1972	Hubert Levels (Hol)	1996	Alan Scotthorne (Eng)
1973	Pierre Michiels (Bel)	1997	Alan Scotthorne (Eng)
1974	Aribert Richter (FRG)	1998	Alan Scotthorne (Eng)
1975	Ian Heaps (Eng)	1999	Bob Nudd (Eng)
1977	Jean Mainil (Bel)	2000	Jacopo Falsini (Ita)
1978	Jean-Pierre Fouquet (Fra)	2001	Umberto Balabeni (Ita)
1979	Gerard Heulard (Fra)	2002	G Blasco (Esp)
1980	Wolf-Rudiger Kremkus (FRG)		

MEN'S TEAM

1957	Italy	1964	France	1971	Italy
1958	Belgium	1965	Romania	1972	France
1959	France	1966	France	1973	Belgium
1960	Belgium	1967	Belgium	1974	France
1961	DR Germany	1968	France	1975	France
1962	Italy	1969	Holland	1976	Italy
1963	France	1970	Belgium	1977	Luxembourg

1978	France	1987	England	1996	Italy
1979	France	1988	England	1997	Italy
1980	FR Germany	1989	Wales	1998	England
1981	France	1990	France	1999	Spain
1982	Holland	1991	England	2000	Italy
1983	Belgium	1992	Italy	2001	England
1984	Luxembourg	1993	Italy	2002	Portugal
1985	England	1994	England		
1986	Italy	1995	France		

Four-times individual world coarse fishing champion, Bob Nudd.

WORLD FLY-FISHING CHAMPIONSHIPS

Year	Host nation	Individual	Team
1981	Luxembourg	C. Wittkamp (Hol)	Holland
1982	Spain	V. Diez y Diez (Spa)	Italy
1983	Italy	F. Alvarez (Spa)	Italy
1984	Spain	A. Pawson (Eng)	Italy
1985	Poland	L. Frasik (Pol)	Poland
1986	Belgium	S. Svoboda (Cz)	Italy
1987	England	B. Leadbetter (Eng)	England
1988	Australia	J. Pawson (Eng)	England
1989	Finland	W. Trzebiunia (Pol)	Poland
1990	Wales	F. Szajnik (Pol)	Czechoslovakia
1991	New Zealand	B. Leadbetter (Eng)	New Zealand
1992	Italy	P. Cocito (Ita)	Italy
1993	Canada	R. Owen (Wal)	England
1994	Norway	P. Cognard (Fra)	Czech Republic
1995	Ireland	J. Herman (Eng)	England
1996	Czech Republic	P. Cocito (Ita)	Czech Republic
1997	USA	P. Cognard (Fra)	France
1998	Poland	T. Starychfojtu (Cz)	Czech Republic
1999	Australia	R. Stuart (Aus)	Australia
2000	England	P. Cognard (Fra)	France
2001	Sweden	V. Sedivy (Czech)	France

Eric Good fishing for rainbow trout on Butterstone Loch, Perthshire.

WORLD SHORE CHAMPIONSHIPS

Men's Individual

1996	Chris Clark (Eng)	Steve Allmark (Eng)	Stewart Cresswell (Sco)
1997	Joe Arch (Wal)	Steve Allmark (Eng)	Jimmy Jones (Wal)
2002	Alan Price (Wal)	Ricardo Silva (Por)	Mario Verissimo (Por)

Men's Team

1993	Spain	France	Portugal
1996	England	Scotland	Belgium
1997	Wales	England	Scotland
2002	Portugal	Wales	England

WORLD BOAT CHAMPIONSHIPS

Individual

1996	Bruno Cocciolo (Ita)	Rodger Symonds (Eng)	Joachiam Balzunat (Ger)
1997	Tim Pressley (Eng)	Paul Cartwright (Eng)	Jackie Gevaert (Bel)
2002	Ronny De Ranter (Bel)	Gabriel Borges (Esp)	Rolf Marschalek (Eng)

Team

1996	Germany	Italy	England
1997	Germany	Slovenia	Ireland
2002	Spain	Belgium	France

*Below: Photographer Ken Towner
fishing in Ireland.
Opposite: Fishing at a lake near
Wellington in the seventies.*

WOMEN and FISHING

Although angling remains a predominantly male preoccupation, there are undoubtedly historical precedents as far back as Dame Juliana Berners, the Prioress of St Albans who published a seminal work on fly-fishing in 1496. More recently, since the 1970s at least, more and more women have begun to take up the sport and are perhaps now regarded as equal to their male counterparts. Indeed, according to many sources women prove to excel at angling and some studies suggest that for some reason, possibly connected to pheromones, our natural scent, that women actually catch larger fish. Such claims certainly seem to be borne out in the case of salmon, with the current British rod-caught record having been set by a woman, Georgina Ballantine, as far back as 1922. Her 64lb specimen also ranks as the largest ever authenticated fish caught in freshwater in the UK. Also noteworthy is the 17lb 8oz record for a small-eyed ray, caught in the Bristol Channel and set in 1991 by first-time female angler Mrs Sue Storey.

GREAT PATIENCE

Although women tend to take up fishing later in life than men, many enjoying their first outing accompanying a partner or spouse, those that do are frequently instantly hooked, finding that they can indeed hold their own against male competition. Some have argued that women have a greater capacity for patience than do many men, but the more active pursuit of fly or game fishing attracts women in even greater numbers than either coarse or

sea fishing, and many women themselves put their talent down to their dexterity and finesse, for where men usually fish more aggressively, brute force alone is seldom a prerequisite for landing even a large fish.

NATIONAL CHAMPIONSHIPS

Since the mid-70s women have firmly established themselves as a presence in angling, holding their own National Championships and developing a great many local and regional clubs and societies, in fact it seems that on the whole, women tend to pursue fishing as more of a social activity than men, often fishing together in groups, unlike the (albeit somewhat stereotypical) lone male angler. However, when it comes to fishing with and against men in mixed competition, there too women have continued to prove that there is nothing to stop them from rivalling and outperforming the boys.

Below: The Queen Mother, 70, salmon fishing on the River Dee in Aberdeenshire. Despite being an expert angler her catch was nil. She fished for two hours before returning to Birkhall, near Ballater where she was spending a ten-day holiday.

Opposite: Georgina Ballantine still holds the current British rod-caught record for a trout set as far back as 1922. Her 64lb specimen also ranks as the largest ever authenticated fish caught in freshwater in the UK.

WOMEN'S INDIVIDUAL COARSE CHAMPIONSHIPS

1997   Wendy Locker (Eng)
           Dominique Miseeri (Fra)
           Sandra Haikon-Hunt (Eng)
1999   Gillian Foy (Eng)
           Wendy Lythgoe (Eng)

WOMEN'S TEAM COARSE CHAMPIONSHIPS

| 1997 | England | France | Italy |
| 1999 | England | Poland | Italy |

WOMEN'S INDIVIDUAL SHORE CHAMPIONSHIPS

1997 Natasha Frtovic (Cro)
       Heide-Marie Hansen (Ger)
       Jane Elliot (Wal)
2002 Maria Valente (Por)
       Andreina Grasso (Ita)
       Flavia Santoro (Ita)

WOMEN'S TEAM SHORE CHAMPIONSHIPS

1993	Spain	France	Germany
1997	France	England	Wales
2002	Italy	Portugal	Croatia

Above: Lynn Warner fishing in Colchester. 'The only time men have an advantage is when you have to cast a long way out, or when fishing for carp which fight a lot.'
Right: A delightful setting at Chipstead, Kent.
Opposite: Fashion for country weekend fishing.

A FISHING MISCELLANY

'ALL FISHERMEN ARE LIARS
EXCEPT YOU AND ME AND TO TELL YOU THE TRUTH,
I'M NOT SO SURE ABOUT YOU!'

A ngling has traditionally given rise to tall tales, if not outright lies, mainly about gargantuan specimens which managed to evade capture, for as someone once said 'nothing grows faster than a fish from the time it bites until the time it gets away'. However, fishing also throws up its fair share of eccentric and unusual moments that have actually happened. Here are some of those weird and wonderful occurrences, featuring some highly unusual techniques documented in photographs… and of course, unlike the fisherman, the camera never lies!

Opposite: A fish hasn't got much of a chance at this stocked pond in Tokyo. Left: Tuning in - John Lee takes his satellite dish and TV when he goes fishing.

PERHAPS WE TOOK THE RIGHT TURN AFTER ALL...

As the salmon rod-fishing season opened on the River Tay in Scotland in 1964, most onlookers would have been stunned to see Mr Ian Cameron, a local businessman, driving downstream in his amphibious car with two friends. Perhaps they would have been further shocked to see one of the passengers, Mr Duncan McGregor, catching an 8lb salmon soon after the traditional opening ceremony.

PIKE BIKE!

A slightly dubious-looking machine, but John Calvert, pictured on his cycle catamaran on the Thames at Goring, Oxfordshire, claims that this is the best way to fish. He found the Victorian contraption underneath his house and using his skills as a classic car restorer, spent six months working on new floats, a rudder and propeller to return it to full working order. Not only does he turn a few heads as he pedals along; Mr Calvert finds this a highly effective angling method, landing a 15lb pike on his first outing, which towed him for some distance before he reeled it in.

FISHERMAN'S BEST FRIEND...

Whilst some dogs might fetch a stick or even retrieve the newspaper, Buster the Boxer dog has developed a particular talent for fishing. Accompanying his owner, 68-year-old Arne Alfredsson on fishing expeditions near the town of Oskarshamn in Sweden, Buster has learned to stand completely still in the water with his mouth submerged and to grab fish in his jaws which he then delivers unharmed to his owner.

CELEBRITY BITES

Getting away from it all - clockwise from the right:

- Diana Rigg at her home near Stirling, Scotland returning from a fishing outing.
- Prince Charles in search of salmon on the River Dee near Balmoral.
- Doug Ellis, Chairman of Aston Villa F.C.
- Golfer Lee Westwood fishing on Loch Lomond after a match.
- Henry Cooper getting away from it all at Wraysbury, Bucks, the day before his heavyweight fight with Joe Erskine at Wembley in 1961.
- Keen fisherman and rugby legend Gareth Edwards.
- Television presenter Jeremy Paxman.

CONSERVATION,
ETIQUETTE and THE LAW

All anglers can commonly be regarded as natural conservationists, for any pastime that involves spending a great deal of time in the natural environment tends to instil an appreciation and respect for its wildlife and their habitats. But fishing can, and at times, usually through inexperience or carelessness, does have a negative impact. It is also of prime importance to remember that anglers are not the only users of our coasts and inland waterways, and that consideration for others should go hand-in-hand with an awareness of conservation. Therefore, it is important to remember and observe certain codes of conduct relating to both of these factors to ensure the protection of fish, other wildlife and the environment itself, to preserve the beauty of the natural world and to ensure the future of fishing. Many of the simple measures here could be regarded as ethical, but it is important too to consider that there are also legal matters relating to the angler and some of these are outlined first.

Competing on Rutland Water

ANGLING AND THE LAW

LICENCES

Anyone over the age of twelve is required by law to hold a valid Rod Fishing Licence if they wish to use a rod and line to fish for coarse or game fish in England and Wales. No such restrictions apply to sea fishing from the shore; however, there may be restrictions pertaining to access and to particularly busy beaches or conservation areas. Also, structures such as piers and breakwaters are usually privately or council owned and it may be necessary to obtain permission to fish from certain sites.

In the case of freshwater fishing, licences may be obtained from the Environment Agency and are available in post offices. It is then usually necessary to purchase a permit to fish a particular water; these are often available as day tickets, and should be bought from the relevant fishery owner or angling club. Recently a Beginners' Licence has been introduced to support coaching schemes, which is valid for a twenty-four-hour period of tuition and is obtained from coaching organisations themselves.

CLOSE SEASONS

The national coarse fish close season covers 15th March – 15th June inclusive, and applies to all rivers and streams in England and Wales, but excludes most stillwaters and canals. The purpose of the close season is to protect fish during the breeding season and although there may be fluctuations in spawning times, it generally proves to be effective. Close seasons also go some way to minimise disturbance to waters and bankside habitats and may be beneficial to other recreational water users. In the case of stillwaters, which are usually managed and restocked, no such season is necessary, and after extensive study it appears that year-round canal fishing also has little impact. There are however some exceptions, and water authorities or private owners may impose their own close seasons on particular waters, especially in the case of Sites of Special Scientific Interest. In the case of trout and salmon fishing similar byelaws apply. There is no close season for non-migratory rainbow trout in stillwaters, but elsewhere local byelaws apply and there are close seasons in all waters applied to brown trout which also vary from location to location. With regard to salmon, only artificial flies or lures may be used before 16th June, and any salmon caught before this date must be returned immediately. The Environment Agency also promotes catch and return throughout the year in order to try to safeguard stocks.

ANGLING
and the ENVIRONMENT

HANDLING FISH

Whether returning your fish, or in the case of sea or game fishing keeping it, minimisation of suffering must be paramount. At sea there are also legal restrictions on returning undersized fish, details of which should be obtained from your local Sea Fisheries Committee. If choosing to keep and eat your catch it should be dispatched as quickly as possible with a clean blow to the head.

When handling fish always do so with wet hands, and if returning them to the water try to do so as quickly as possible. A disgorger for the effective removal of hooks should form part of any self-respecting fisherman's tackle and the proper use of it should be learnt. If wishing to weigh or photograph a catch, always hold the fish firmly to prevent dropping it and have cameras and weighing equipment close at hand before landing. Never hold a fish under its gill covers, or use a gaff if it is to be returned, rather, a landing net should be used to support the fish when bringing it out of the water.

A landing net is a useful aid and helps to avoid damaging fish. Once landed your catch should be held securely with wet hands.

BREAKAGES, LOSS OF LINE
OR TACKLE & LITTER

It is important to try to minimise the loss of tackle as lost weights and lines can pose a threat to wildlife for many years. Nylon monofilament line does not degrade easily and it presents a particular risk for birds and animals, therefore it is recommended that anglers attempt to ensure the use of appropriate tackle, i.e. line of the correct breaking strain, and to regularly check the condition of lines. Some snagging and breaking is almost unavoidable, but where possible broken lines should be retrieved, and when coarse fishing, if tackle cannot be recovered, it should be reported to fishery owners or club bailiffs. Discarded line should be disposed of by means of burning or cut into short lengths. Always clear up before leaving a venue that you have been fishing and remove any litter that you notice whether it is yours or not.

POLLUTION

Generally, our seas and inland waterways are cleaner than they have been for many years, with species returning to shorelines and rivers after long absences, or in other cases, thriving where they have previously never flourished. However, whilst heavy industry may have declined, and the public has become more aware of environmental issues, isolated incidents of pollution continue to be a problem.

Pollution, items washed ashore and sick or injured animals should be reported to the Environment Agency. Although not necessarily angling-related, these could be indicative of serious problems at the water.

Opposite: The Greater London Council's sponsored fishing experiment in the seventies aimed to show the London Thames as a cleaner fishable river.
Above: As rivers such as the Thames become cleaner, catches like this 8lb salmon, caught by Terry Smith in 1995, are becoming more common in built-up areas.

UNATTENDED RODS, HOOKS, WEIGHTS & WILDFOWL

It is an offence to leave a rod unattended when fishing. Doing so may result in unnecessary harm being caused to fish or to wildfowl which may become entangled or attempt to take bait. Leaving baited hooks out of the water poses a similar threat to bankside animals and hooks should be secured to the rod.

If planning to return your catches it is advisable to always use barbless hooks, they minimise damage to fish, and should a bird or other animal be hooked then they are far easier to remove. Birds are perhaps most at risk from discarded tackle, but can also be attracted to surface baits or become entangled during fishing, therefore take great care and attempt to submerge lines and surface baits if birds approach them. Lead weights ingested by birds, particularly swans, used to be a major problem; however, it is now illegal to use lead weights, other than those of sizes 14 − 8 (up to 0.06grams), and those over one ounce.

When sea fishing, particularly when collecting baits, attempt to avoid disturbing wildfowl which are roosting or feeding, especially during winter months when birds are conserving energy.

Below: A solitary angler casts his line over the calm waters of the River Mourne as evening comes to County Tyrone, Ireland. Opposite: One swan happy to regard fishermen as friends, taking a bite from Robert Taylor of Kingston as he fishes at Teddington Lock.

USEFUL CONTACTS

National swan sanctuary
Hotline: 0700 SWAN UK or
01784 431667

RSPCA: 08705 555999

Wildlife Hospital Trust:
01844 292292

BAIT

Sea anglers often collect their own baits such as marine worms, crabs or shellfish from the shore, and when doing so there are a number of things to bear in mind. Always backfill holes from which bait has been dug in order to protect the habitat for other marine wildlife and to reduce risks for other users of the shore, for example avoid digging around boat moorings and slipways. If collecting crabs, always replace rocks and vegetation carefully, to prevent other animals from being exposed or crushed, and never take those carrying eggs, or undersized edible specimens. It is important too, to avoid collecting too much bait. Unless it is to be properly disposed of or taken home and stored, discarded bait can be unpleasant for others, and taking too much may threaten eco-systems. When buying bait, one should be sure to use only native species to avoid the possibility of introducing species or parasites which may upset the natural balance of native habitats.

This rule also applies to using live or dead baits in freshwater fishing; in fact, fish taken for this reason may only be used as bait in the water from which they have been caught. Crayfish may never be used, and new byelaws prevent the use of freshwater fish as bait in most of England's Lake District, partly to prevent possible contamination, but also to protect some rarer species such as the vendace, schelly and arctic char from fish which may compete for food and also eat their eggs.

Mr Hall of Farnham Angling Club landing a good-sized roach in 1936.

CONSERVATION AREAS

The public right to fish recreationally along our coastlines extends to wildlife conservation sites, but anglers should therefore be particularly mindful when fishing in such areas in order to protect natural habitats and species which are already deemed to be rare or vulnerable. There are also specific fish conservation sites designated as nurseries and the responsible angler should familiarise him or herself with conservation areas, information on which can be obtained from English Nature and local Sea Fisheries Committees.

GLOSSARY of TERMS

ARLESEY BOMB	A pear-shaped ledgering weight attached to a swivel.
BALE ARM	The moveable arm found on a fixed-spool reel which revolves around the spool to wind in the line.
BITE ALARM	An audible electronic bite indicator, particularly useful for ledgering or for night fishing when floats may not be visible.
BIVVY	Derived from bivouac, a small, usually open-fronted tent or shelter.
BOOTLACE	A term for young eels or elvers.
BREAKING STRAIN	A manufacturer's guide as to the potential strength of fishing line.
CENTRE-PIN	A winch-like reel, the precursor of fixed-spool types, which features a central spindle. Most commonly used in fly and sea fishing.
COFFIN LEAD	A coffin-shaped ledgering weight.
DAPPING	A fly-fishing technique, delivering a dry fly with the help of the wind in such a manner that it will bounce across the surface of the water.
DEADBAITING	The practice of using dead fish to catch predatory species.
DISGORGER	A device used to remove a hook from a fish's mouth.
DRIFTING	In sea fishing, allowing bait to drift with the tide when fishing from an un-anchored boat.
DRY FLY	An artificial fly designed to sit on the surface of the water.
FIXED-SPOOL	Type of reel with a fixed, forward-facing spool which enables easier and longer casting. See also bale arm.
FORCEPS	Implement used instead of a disgorger, for the removal of larger hooks.
FOUL-HOOKED	Term used to describe the accidental hooking of a fish in a fin or anywhere other than in the mouth. A fish caught in such a way cannot be considered for record status.
FRY	Recently hatched fish or fish larvae.
GRILSE	Term given to a young salmon returning from the sea to spawn after one year.

Opposite: 'A good angler must have plenty of hope and patience, with a searching and observing wit', wrote Izaak Walton more than 300 years ago. In modern times he could add a healthy bank balance to cope with the high cost of fishing tackle. This display of tackle by Stan Elkington is what the complete angler required 20 years ago.

GROUNDBAIT	A dry mixture of ingredients such as breadcrumbs, made into a paste with water and rolled into balls to be thrown or catapulted into a swim to attract fish.
KEEPNET	A cylindrical net, sealed at one end for retaining fish. Keepnets should only be used when it is a necessity that fish be held for a short while, for example during match fishing, and must be of suitable knotless material to avoid damage to the fish.
KELT	A salmon or sea-trout returning to the sea after spawning, usually in poor condition as a result.
LANDING NET	A long-handled net used to safely land hooked fish.
LATERAL LINE	The main sensory organ of a fish, located along the flanks.
LEDGERING	Fishing with weights to present bait at the bottom of a swim.
LIVEBAITING	The practice of using small, freshly caught fish as bait when fishing for predatory species.
LOOSEFEED	Bait such as maggots or groundbait thrown into an area to encourage fish to feed and to remain feeding around the hook bait.
LURE	Any large artificial bait or fly, usually designed to represent small fish. May be quite a crude arrangement of feathers, especially in sea fishing, though the range is vast and diverse.
MARGIN FISHING	Angling very close to the bankside without weights, usually for carp, catfish and other species which feed in the shallows.
MULTIPLIER	Sea-fishing reel in which a system of gears multiplies the revolutions of the spool enabling long shore casts, and when winding, easing the strain on an angler. Useful from boats when catching large specimens.
OLIVETTE	An oval or teardrop-shaped weight used instead of split shot when angling with a pole.
PARR	A young game fish, particularly salmon, not yet ready to spawn.
PLUG	A type of lure used in coarse fishing, designed to imitate the small fish eaten by predators such as pike.
PLUMMET (& PLUMBING)	A cork-bottomed weight used in conjunction with a float, attached to the hook when 'plumbing' a swim, that is, gauging the depth of an area to be fished.
PRIEST	A small but heavy cosh, used in game and sea fishing to kill a fish which is intended to be eaten. Should be delivered cleanly and swiftly to the back of the fish's head.

QUIVERTIP	Bite indicator used when ledgering that takes the form of a flexible tip attatched to the end of the rod.
SHOT / SPLIT SHOT	Small spherical weights attached to the line to balance floats.
SMOLT	A salmon or other game fish which has reached the migratory stage of its development.
SPINNING	The practice of using spinning lures to attract fish, often performed when fishing from the shore and particularly effective when fishing for mackerel.
SPOOL	The central drum of a reel onto which line is wound.
SPOONS	Type of spoon-shaped lure designed for flatfish angling.
SPRINGER	Term given to a spawning salmon freshly arrived in a river from the sea.
STRIKE	The act of jerking a rod to ensure that a biting fish is secured.
SWIM	The specific area of water being fished.
SWIMFEEDER	A small device used when ledgering to release loose feed into a swim.
SWINGTIP	A bite indicator, very much like a quivertip but far more sensitive, and as such only suitable for stillwater.
SWIVEL	A small linking device with an eyelet at each end of a central barrel, allowing tackle to rotate independently without twisting the line.
TERMINAL TACKLE	The last part of one's tackle arrangement including the hook and bait.
TROTTING	To allow bait to drift downstream or downtide in rivers, estuaries or from the shore.
UNHOOKING MAT	Mat upon which a fish may be more safely unhooked.
WADERS	Waterproof boots reaching to thigh or chest.
WAGGLER	Type of float attached only at the base and secured with shot.
WATERCRAFT	The skill of reading the water to identify appropriate swims and to employ the best methods for fishing them.
WET FLY	An artificial fly designed to sink below the surface.

ACKNOWLEDGEMENTS

The photographs in this book are from the archives of the *Daily Mail*.
Particular thanks to
Steve Torrington, Dave Sheppard, Brian Jackson,
Alan Pinnock, Richard Jones and all the staff.

Thanks also to
Cliff Salter, Maureen Hill, Corinne Hill, Carol Salter,
Murray Mahon, Eric Good, Frances Hill, Peter Wright,
Trevor Bunting and Simon Taylor.
Design by John Dunne.

Many thanks to the British Record (rod-caught) Fish
Committee and the National Federation of Sea Anglers
for their help with the statistics and records

The publisher would like to thank
Oxford Scientific Films and the photographers for permission
to reproduce their pictures on the following pages:
30 Keith Ringland; 35, 41, 44 Colin Milkin; 36 Peter Gathercole; 38/9, 83 OSF;
40, 75 Paulo De Oliveira; 42/3, 46/7 52/3 Hans Reinhard; 46/7, 61 Max Gibbs;
64 Steve Littlewood; 73 Sue Scott; 71, 77 Paul Kay; 87 Michael Leach